FALLEN ANGELS

FALLEN ANGELS

RITA LORENA LINK

TCU PRESS
Fort Worth, Texas

Library of Congress Cataloging-in-Publication Data

Names: Link, Rita Lorena author
Title: Fallen angels / by: Rita Lorena Link.
Description: Fort Worth : TCU Press, [2026] | Includes bibliographical references and index.
Identifiers: LCCN 2025052576 (print) | LCCN 2025052577 (ebook) | ISBN 9780875659619 paperback | ISBN 9780875659626 ebook
Subjects: LCSH: Link, Rita Lorena--Childhood and youth | Adopted children--Texas--Waggoner Ranch--Biography | Ranch life--Texas--Waggoner Ranch | W.T. Waggoner Ranch (Tex.)--History | W.T. Waggoner Ranch (Tex.)--Social life and customs | W.T. Waggoner Ranch (Tex.)--Biography | Texas--Biography | LCGFT: Autobiographies | Biographies
Classification: LCC F391.4.L56 A3 2026 (print) | LCC F391.4.L56 (ebook)
LC record available at https://lccn.loc.gov/2025052576
LC ebook record available at https://lccn.loc.gov/2025052577

TCU PRESS

TCU Box 298300
Fort Worth, Texas 76129
www.tcupress.com

Design by Bill Brammer

REPRESENTED BY
Anne G. Devlin
Max Gartenberg Literary Agency
912 N. Pennsylvania Ave.
Yardley, PA 19067

TEL: 215-295-9230
E-MAIL: agdevlin@aol.com
www.maxgartenberg.com

FOREWORD

Of all the characters in this story, one deserves to be introduced separately, and right here, at the beginning: the W. T. Waggoner Ranch. It occupies eight hundred square miles of north Texas, roughly the size of Los Angeles and New York City combined.

In the years since its founding, miles of newsprint have been dedicated to this saga, but none of them have shone a light on what I call the soul of the ranch—the lives of thousands of men, women, children, and animals who thrived together on this enormously bountiful land through wars and recoveries, high times and low, loves, rivalries, betrayals, births, deaths and aftermaths, just like the rest of the world.

As I begin telling this story, and for the purposes of a comprehensive introduction to this character, here are some examples of how the press has portrayed Waggoner Ranch in recent years, including its current status:

The Texas Monthly published a long piece by Gary Cartwright in January 2004 detailing the founding of the ranch and the familial intrigue that led to its eventual downfall:

> Northwest Texas was open range in the 1850's, when Dan Waggoner and his fifteen-year-old black slave trailed 242 Longhorn cattle and 6 horses to Wise County. Hostile Comanches and Kiowas, plus a few foolhardy nesters trying to scratch out a living, occupied this endless stretch of grassland . . . Waggoner, a widower, and his young son, William Thomas, settled on Catlett Creek, near present-day Decatur. As the frontier pushed westward, he expanded his herd and bought more land, in Clay and Wichita counties. In 1869 Dan made seventeen-year-old W. T. a full partner, gave him $12, a group of drovers, and fifty hard-used saddle horses, and sent him to Abilene, Kansas, with a herd of five thousand steers . . . That became the seed money for the Waggoner empire.

This next passage from the same article describes how the epic family feud began and will help make sense of a conversation I have with Daddy later in the book:

> W. T. Waggoner had built a great ranch, but in 1909 he was 57 years old and thinking about its future. The squabbling that has ensnared the ranch for almost a century began on Christmas Day of that year, when W. T. divided the ranch that he and his dad had founded into four large tracts. He kept the east side of the ranch, called White Face, for himself.
>
> . . . Now the sun is going down on the Waggoner Ranch, perhaps forever. I ask him (G. L. Proctor, 79-year-old former Waggoner Ranch foreman, now retired) what he thinks of the family feud that threatens to end the way of life that he knew. "It doesn't seem real to even think about it," he says. "The only thing I can figure, it was given to them. Didn't any of them have to work or suffer to get it. That's the only reason anyone would want to sell."

I was fifty-nine when this article was published. I felt a resigned disappointment remembering that Mother and I were just two small pieces of collateral damage in the long chess game over control of the ranch. Growing up there I heard all the stories of the backbiting and saw the feud between the two sides of the family firsthand, but still, I always imagined that my stepbrother, Bucky, and I would run the ranch together with our families one day. Knowing now how it all shook out, I can't help but wonder if we were the lucky ones to get out when we did, even if we were forced to do so.

On July 21, 2015, Bloomberg News Service announced that the ranch was up for sale:

> FOR SALE: Largest ranch in the U.S. within a single fence. Texas fixer-upper with more than 1,000 oil wells; 6,800 head of cattle; 500 quarter horses; 30,000 acres of cropland; tombstones for legendary cowboys, long-dead dogs, and a horse buried standing up. Favorite of Will Rogers and Teddy Roosevelt. Colorful history of drinking and divorce. Fifteen-minute drive to rib eyes at the Rusty Spur in Vernon. Ideal for Saudi oil sheiks, billionaire

> hedge funders, and dot commers who can tell a cow from a steer. Profitable. Zero debt. Property taxes only $800,000 a year. Price: $725 million.

The tone of the announcement may have been tongue-in-cheek, but it was also dead right, especially the bit about a colorful history of drinking and divorce. I worried for the ranch and crossed my fingers, hoping it would be bought by someone who could love it and care for it as I had seen it cared for by Daddy.

The Dallas Morning News, announcing the sale of the ranch to Stan Kroenke, February 20, 2016, wrote:

> More than 900 would-be buyers came calling. A half-dozen paid $15 million to submit a bid.
>
> . . . On February 10, the once-warring descendants of Tom Waggoner inked a deal transferring ownership of the legendary estate to billionaire Stan Kroenke, owner of the Los Angeles Rams and Denver Nuggets. The sale (at $725 million) vaulted Kroenke into the No. 5 spot among landowners in the U.S.

Hearing the news of the sale was bittersweet. I silently wished Mr. Kroenke all the luck in the world and prayed that the land and the animals were in good hands. I also hoped that the long years of fighting and resentment would fade into history and that a new, long overdue era of peace would come to my childhood home.

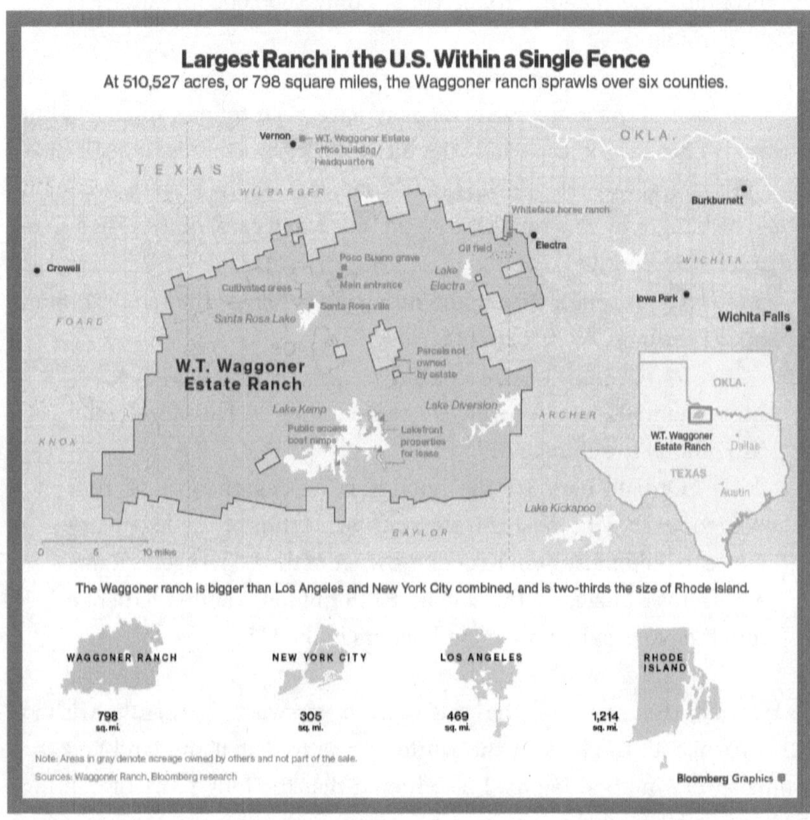
Largest Ranch in the U.S. Within a Single Fence
At 510,527 acres, or 798 square miles, the Waggoner ranch sprawls over six counties.
Vernon
W.T. Waggoner Estate office building/ headquarters
TEXAS
OKLA.
WILBARGER
Burkburnett
Whiteface horse ranch
Electra
Oil field
Poco Bueno grave
Main entrance
Lake Electra
Crowell
Cultivated areas
Santa Rosa villa
Santa Rosa Lake
FOARD
WICHITA
Iowa Park
Wichita Falls
W.T. Waggoner Estate Ranch
Parcels not owned by estate
Lake Kemp
Lake Diversion
ARCHER
Public access boat ramps
Lakefront properties for lease
KNOX
Lake Kickapoo
BAYLOR
0
5
10 miles
OKLA.
W.T. Waggoner Estate Ranch
Dallas
TEXAS
Austin
The Waggoner ranch is bigger than Los Angeles and New York City combined, and is two-thirds the size of Rhode Island.
WAGGONER RANCH
798 sq. mi.
NEW YORK CITY
305 sq. mi.
LOS ANGELES
469 sq. mi.
RHODE ISLAND
1,214 sq. mi.
Note: Areas in gray denote acreage owned by others and not part of the sale.
Sources: Waggoner Ranch, Bloomberg research
Bloomberg Graphics

PROLOGUE

Gazing out over the vast Texas landscape, I am struck once again by the raw beauty that lies sprawled before me. Only a Texan, born and raised in this unforgiving land, would agree with my perception. The untrained eye would only see a barren expanse of red dirt punctuated by thorny mesquite trees. Sitting by the hilltop pond that provides the lush, green oasis for our home, I am filled with a deep, abiding love for this land because my roots are here, deep in the ground, tying me to everyone and everything I love in life. Blue skies go on forever, draped with fleecy, white clouds that change shape constantly, creating a menagerie of shifting animals. Deep gullies reflect shades of red, gold, and brown as the sun moves slowly across the sky.

To the south stand the huge, old cottonwood, oak, and sycamore trees that shade the lazy stream beneath Hoot 'N Hollar Bridge. Picnics here are heaven, dangling my feet and sending tiny leaf boats floating downstream, wondering what their fate might be. To the west are fields of wheat and maize that sway and ripple like golden seas as the wind gently ebbs and flows around them. My horse always breaks into a trot in his eagerness to reach the knobby, green horse apples that await him in the trees beside those fields. The barns, shops, and animal pens lie to the northwest, flanked by huge gardens and orchards that bountifully supply us with almost all of our food. Summer harvest is a time of shelling peas and shucking corn, as succulent smells of boiling jelly waft through the house.

To the north is the duck tank where thousands of ducks and geese stop for food and water on their journey south each year. Surrounding the tank is the Prairie Dog Town, which my father guarded with the fierceness of a mother hen. Everyone on the ranch knew there would be dire consequences for anyone caught killing the prairie dogs or the white-tailed deer that lived near Hoot 'N Hollar Bridge.

To the east lie the oil fields where the black gold is produced and which, for good or ill, became the lifeblood of the ranch. On a still night, I could hear the regular thumping of the pump jacks, like a giant heartbeat emanating from the earth. Oil is a rank-smelling, ecologically destructive substance, but it did bring us great wealth, both in terms of money and family stories. Texas crude oil turned my grandmother Electra Waggoner into an infamous international playgirl who could spend it as fast as they could pump it. She almost single-handedly supported Neiman Marcus, spending as much as ten thousand dollars a week according to legend and could throw a party you would never forget. Party favors at her house included pistols used for target practice on the chandelier, and the town of Electra was named after her when she and her entire party jumped into the oil canals of her latest "gusher." She and Daddy's father had matching doves tattooed on their buttocks while on their honeymoon in Paris, and I always thought the bird of peace was a strange choice for a girl who lived so hard and died so young.

I cannot think of this great land without imputing its partner in crime, the quicksilver Texas weather. Each season unleashes a power of nature that would rival the apocalypse. Ferocious thunderstorms produce hail the size of baseballs. Tornadoes come out of nowhere to follow their perennial path down Tornado Alley, roaring like a gigantic freight train after the deadly calm before the storm. The sky turns an angry, dark green and the air is charged with a pregnant waiting. Your heart begins to pound, and you feel more alive than you ever thought possible. Lying in a ditch, watching a tornado suck your car up into its ravenous mouth is a thrill hard to match. The blistering hot dust storms can take the paint off your house or the skin off your bones. The ice storms create magical, glittering forests of beauty before the weight begins to splinter the giant trees into deadly instruments of destruction.

The wildlife in Texas is as intriguing as the weather. There are mosquitos big enough to carry you off, not to mention the fire ants, scorpions, tarantulas, water moccasins, and rattlesnakes. To this day, even when I am in New York City, I watch my feet, an embarrassing habit acquired from years of looking out for rattlers. I never got to hear the howl of the wolves because they were exterminated not long after President Teddy Roosevelt came to the ranch for an event that came to be known as The Great Wolf Hunt.

My favorite critters are the wily coyotes, and I love lying in bed at night listening to them sing. It is a lonely, mournful sound, but it gives me comfort and lets me know all is right with the world. My feelings are not shared by most ranchers, who typically hate coyotes with a rabid passion. Most of the men I know, including my father, keep a gun in the car just in case they get lucky enough to kill one and then hang the carcass on a fence post as a warning to other coyotes. I always found this practice to be an abomination and would ban it if circumstances were different and I were in charge.

If I were in charge! That thought brings me out of my reverie and I feel as if an avalanche of emotions is going to crush me. This is not the ending I pictured as a child when I sat here dreaming of my Prince Charming. My brother and I planned to run the ranch together, with both of our families living here in harmony. Instead, we are not in charge, there is no Prince Charming, and my brother and I are locked in a brutal court battle. Today I must leave my beloved ranch. I must sever my roots here and try to survive the loss of all I hold dear.

CHAPTER 1

Lu and Charles Meet

I THROW A PEBBLE INTO THE POND, and as I watch the ripples spread out from the point of contact, I realize life works much the same way. Seemingly insignificant choices have a ripple effect on all those who follow, sometimes profoundly influencing the lives of hundreds of people. As I think back on all of the choices made by my parents that have brought me to this crossroad, I don't know whether to laugh or cry. They were players in a time when the world had gone mad and teetered on the brink of destruction. World War II had given rise to a new motto fully embraced by the war-weary pleasure seekers of their generation: *Live and love today, for tomorrow we may die!*

Dallas, Texas, was the perfect playground for anyone seeking money and pleasure. It was a boomtown where the oil barons and the cattle barons created the most lavish and decadent lifestyles imaginable. Old money met new money and everyone mingled and thrived in a hothouse of prosperity.

Fort Worth, on the other hand, was ruled by old money aristocrats who turned up their noses at the nouveau riche upstarts across the Trinity River. All the new money in the world could not get you accepted into the social circles of the "Cowtown Elite." Both my father and my stepfather were members of Fort Worth's crème de la crème, but they preferred to forsake their stuffy heritage for the more glamorous potpourri being created across the Trinity. In Dallas, wealthy bachelors lived in penthouses atop grand hotels like The Stoneleigh and threw lavish parties that lasted for days. Neiman Marcus models and showgirls from Las Vegas were the main attraction at these galas, backed up by famous big bands flown in from all over the country. It was to this Texas hotbed of high life, with all its succulent temptations, that my parents were drawn like moths to a flame.

My mother and my biological father met at a party in the grand ballroom of the Melrose Hotel. I can only imagine the spontaneous combustion that must have occurred when those two heartbreakers set eyes on each other. Both were newly divorced and looking for their next conquest. Neither of them knew it, but they had both met their match.

My father, Charles Payne Link, was a slender five-foot-eleven, with black wavy hair and seductive green eyes. He was famous for his flashing, white smile and devastating charm. Both men and women adored him, and he was considered to be the handsomest man in Dallas. My mother was his eighth and last wife, and the only one who did not attend his funeral years later. Charles's father was a wealthy doctor in Fort Worth, and after his death, Charles had no strong direction. He easily manipulated his adoring mother, whose tastes were as extravagant as his own. He was close with all of the up-and-coming oil barons of Dallas, and what he lacked in wealth he made up for with charisma. He was a magnet to women, and as such, his main function within the group was to procure Neiman Marcus models and other young ingénues for the parties. This role was a tremendous asset to his business dealings with his oil buddies, but it was not terribly conducive to maintaining a happy marriage. Predictably, this talent was to be his contribution to the inevitable split between him and my mother.

My mother, Lula Judd, was a small, slender blonde with provocative brown eyes. Her startling beauty was equaled only by her vivacious personality, and it was said she could charm the bark right off a tree. In later years, I came to think of her as the "Fatal Flower," but in those days, she revealed only the sweet warmth of a country girl that, combined with her beauty, made her irresistible. Her father had been a successful farmer in Vernon, Texas, and her lack of city sophistication made her even more desirable to the wealthy men of Dallas. Perhaps that was because it was such a delight to introduce her to a world she had only dreamed of but knew she belonged in. These jaded men were like gods in the eyes of girls like my mother, and they paid homage to each other out of awe and gratitude, deeply appreciative for what each brought to the table. No one ever gave a thought to what would happen when these girls grew accustomed to the life of the rich and famous and no longer regarded their husbands as gods. It was in this Cinderella climate that Lu and Charles met one another, got married, and quickly became the reigning beautiful couple of Dallas.

It wasn't long before the hidden flaws behind their beautiful facade began to rip apart an apparently perfect marriage. Neglected by a busy father and spoiled by an indulgent mother, Charles was the essence of sweet, genuine charm but was terribly lacking in any real business acumen. It became painfully clear that he was not nearly as solvent as appearances or the company he kept would indicate. Like many young men raised with great wealth, he had no idea how to make money. He certainly knew how to spend it, however, and flagrantly lived way beyond his means, which led to a dependence on his mother and his friends. She was quite the spendthrift herself: It was not unusual for her to sell land, stock, and even jewelry to indulge his whims. His friends regarded him as the most genuinely nice gentleman they knew and rightly assessed his talents to be his charm and character rather than his money-making abilities. Consequently, they generously included him in occasional oil deals set up by the audacious *wild-catters*, those rough-and-ready oil men who were hungry and not afraid to gamble.

It seemed a fair exchange to them—his gifts of breeding, good looks, and prowess with women in return for their monetary patronage. This was a very workable arrangement for everyone except my mother. She resented her mother-in-law's control and was appalled by Charles's lack of business sense. Her father was a self-made man, and although he was not wealthy by Dallas standards, it was said you could put him on a pile of rocks in the middle of nowhere and he would figure out a way to make money from it. She felt embarrassed and insecure about their financial predicament, and like most of their friends, turned increasingly to liquor to quell her fears.

Unfortunately, she became pregnant with me right away, which only exacerbated the situation. Their financial problems became a glaring threat to her nesting instincts and, even more importantly, she hated being pregnant because it diminished her allure with men. Her husband's function among their male friends was well known to Lu, and as her hormones raged her insecurities kept pace. She obsessed more and more about the constant parties, and the more she complained, the more he was gone and the more she drank. It all came to a head one evening not long after I was born. Having waited all night for Charles to come home, in desperation Lu called the hotel where they usually had their parties. Their good friend, Layton Humphrey, answered the phone and quickly assured her Charles was not there. Knowing he was protecting Charles, Lu convinced Layton she knew her husband was there. Layton promised to try to locate Charles and have him call her.

Frustrated by being trapped at home, enraged by Charles's seeming indifference, and by this time more than a little drunk, Lu drove straight to the Melrose Hotel and circled the parking garage until she found Charles's Cadillac. She then proceeded to ram it until the front end of her own car was dragging on the ground and the engine was making coughing noises. Lu chugged home with a victorious smile on her face.

Needless to say, my father did not find it so amusing, and the fights escalated to dangerous proportions. Just before he died, Father told me that he literally feared for his life and thus left the apartment a few days later, never to return. After realizing that he was not coming back and that she could not pay the bills, Lu packed us up and moved back to my grandmother's house in Vernon.

After a few weeks, one of their friends broke down and became an informant: Charles was hiding at the Beverly Hills Hotel while he orchestrated the divorce proceedings at a safe distance. Not one to be daunted by a good challenge, Lu informed my grandmother that she was going to California to retrieve him. My grandmother, an old-fashioned Christian woman, was horrified to think her daughter would chase a man in such an unseemly way, especially since she was a new mother. My grandmother refused to keep me, hoping that would stop my mother, but Lu decided to take me with her. I have movies of my mother, with me in her arms, fearlessly marching onto that airplane to get her man.

It was not to be. The informant, full of remorse for having betrayed Charles's confidence, warned my father that Lu was hot on his trail. After two weeks of fruitless searching, my mother returned to Vernon, bitter and brokenhearted. I am exceedingly grateful that I have no memories of that trip. Lu refused to sign any of the divorce papers sent to her, and so began the long and embattled siege of a marriage that had begun with such starry-eyed hope.

In desperation, my father played his last ace. He called some friends in Vernon and asked them to invite Lu to every party being thrown. This was a stroke of genius, because he knew his wife and her need for people and parties. He was counting on her attracting a new man into her life, which would hopefully give him exactly what he wanted—a divorce. Little did he know how right he was, or who that man would be. Who could have known the far-reaching ripple effect that one phone call would have on all of us, for generations to come?

Rita's mother, Lula Judd Wharton

Rita's biological father, Charles Link

Lula and Charles *(far right)*

CHAPTER 2

Buster and LaRita

My stepfather, Albert Buckman Wharton Jr., known as Buster, was a wealthy rancher, renowned polo player, world-class hunter, and infamous playboy. He was five-foot-nine with an upper torso that boasted his athletic nature. He was extremely handsome when he was young, but years of alcoholism and hard living had begun to take their toll by the time he was forty. It was his serendipitous decision that profoundly affected so many lives and began the ripple effect that was to wash over us like a giant tidal wave. He was dating two very different women, and while on a drunken gambling spree in Reno, he decided to marry whichever woman got to Reno first. One was a doctor from California, and the other was LaRita, a playgirl from New Mexico.

LaRita's mother was quick to see an opportunity, so she put her on an airplane while the level-headed doctor took a train. The rest is history. Buster married LaRita and took her back to live her Cinderella life on his ranch in Texas.

Unfortunately, any resemblance to Cinderella quickly faded within the first year of their marriage. Buster was captain of the world-champion polo team, El Ranchito, and thus traveled frequently. LaRita usually declined to accompany him on those trips, and it was not long before everyone on the ranch, as well as the nearby town of Vernon, knew why she preferred to stay home. The Air Force had opened a flight training base just outside of Vernon during World War II, and many young cadets attended flight school there before being shipped to the front. These brave young men, so dashing in their uniforms, proved to be an irresistible attraction to many young girls in Vernon. It was not uncommon to see caravans of cars filled with hopeful, excited girls cruising the base in the evenings. Even though she was married, LaRita was not immune to the charms of the young pilots. The ranch was enticingly close to the base and the temptation proved to be too strong. It was only a matter of time before Buster became aware of her infidelities. Luckily, he was not a violent man, but this adulterous slap in the face was too much even for a man raised by an international playgirl. LaRita packed up her things and moved back to New Mexico.

Their decision hit a snag, however, when it was discovered that LaRita was pregnant. Buster knew very well that there was a strong possibility that the child was not his, but for reasons of his own, he decided to accept the baby and take LaRita back. However, she had other plans. Upon arriving at the hospital, Buster leaned over to give his wife a kiss and whispered, "We have a beautiful son." Looking back at him with defiant eyes, LaRita said, "*I* have a son."

A few days later, she returned to New Mexico and they were divorced not long afterward. LaRita walked away with a nice settlement and a child support agreement, even though she refused to let the child call Buster "Daddy." Visitations proved to be very difficult, and although Buster begged her year after year to let Bucky live with us, she always refused.

Now that all of the main characters were divorced, the stage was set for two very different men to chart a course that would inextricably bind us together for life. Buster and Charles had grown up together in Fort Worth, Texas, and although they were almost polar opposites in most ways, they shared an important common denominator: their love of women.

Charles, a debonair city boy with exquisite taste in clothes and jewelry, excelled both in the ballroom and in the parlor, and his exploits in the bedroom were the stuff of legends. His manners were impeccable, and enchanting women was both his great gift and delight.

Buster, on the other hand, was the outdoors type, a real man's man. He loved nature, animals, and almost all sports and was not particularly concerned that some wealthy snobs thought he was a flashy country bumpkin. For all of his great wealth, he was a down-to-earth man who did not have a snobbish bone in his body. Living on a ranch had stripped away for him the superficial values of high society, and he knew survival in the country depended upon the goodwill of your neighbors rather than the balance in your checkbook. His greatest weakness was his taste in women. Perhaps his notorious mother shaped his perception of what a desirable woman should be, and if that is the case, beauty and instability ranked high on his list of admired characteristics. I dare say a biographer would be hard-pressed to pinpoint whether it was his family, women, or booze that actually killed him. For whatever reasons, Buster and Charles shared a love of women in general and one woman in particular—Lu.

Rita's stepfather and owner of the Waggoner Ranch, Buster Wharton

CHAPTER 3

Charles and Buster Discuss Lu

Age Two to Three

Charles's plan worked just as he had hoped. Lu was invited to a lot of parties, and at one of them, she met Buster. It was love at first sight for him, but she was simply awestruck by this famous rancher who was said to be one of the richest men in the country. No man had ever left Lu before Charles, and she was still smarting from the humiliation of his rejection. What better way to get even with Charles and redeem herself in the eyes of the world than to be seen dating Buster Wharton!

Nevertheless, as time went by, she was touched by the ardor of his courtship and soon found herself responding to his relentless pursuit. Ever the great hunter, Buster was quick to see the change in his quarry and decided it was time to pay his old friend Charles a visit. He was on his way to Palm Beach, Florida, for a polo match but decided to stop off in Dallas in order to make his intentions regarding Lu clear to Charles.

Buster arranged to meet Charles at his penthouse suite and arrived with a beautiful redhead in tow. After getting the girl comfortably settled at the bar, they returned to the penthouse to seal my fate. On the elevator, Charles winked at Buster and said, "Still like redheads, I see."

Buster, looking slightly uncomfortable, answered with a rueful smile, "Not really. This was something I planned a while back. Just couldn't get out of it."

After offering Buster a drink and lighting his cigarette, Charles leaned back and said, "So what can I do for you, Bus? It sounded urgent on the phone."

Buster sat silently for a moment, and then, looking Charles straight in the eyes, he said, "I met your wife and I want to know what your intentions are. Do you want her back or do you want a divorce?" Charles burst out laughing but quickly suppressed his mirth when he saw the look on Buster's face. "You're dead serious, aren't you?"

Looking a little embarrassed, Buster replied, "Yes, I am."

After quietly appraising his friend, Charles said, "Well, to put you out of your misery as quickly as possible, I will tell you that I emphatically do not want her back and I do want a divorce. In fact, you would be doing me a great service if you could get Lu to cooperate with me. I sent the papers months ago but she refuses to sign them."

Looking steadily at Charles, Buster began to grin. He stood up to shake his hand and said, "Consider it done, ole buddy. Happy to oblige."

Walking Buster to the door, Charles frowned and hesitated before saying, "Bus, we've been friends for a long time, so I think it's only fair to tell you, she's hell on wheels."

Buster grinned again and said, "Well, you know that's just how I like 'em."

Shaking hands once more, they parted without either of them realizing the full magnitude of what had just taken place. Down through the years, both of them would have occasion to think of that meeting and the far-reaching impact it had on so many lives. Another point of contact and the ripple effect moved on.

CHAPTER 4

Lu and Buster Get Married

Age Three

Bus was as good as his word. The divorce was final in three months, and he and Lu were quietly married in a simple ceremony with only a few friends in attendance. Electra's husband, Johnny Biggs, was the best man and Lu's sister, Avis Judd, was the maid-of-honor. They immediately left on a world cruise so that Buster could introduce his new bride to his glamorous friends and their opulent lifestyle. Naturally, Lu was crowned Queen of the Cruise as she basked in all of her newly acquired glory.

Buster truly believed he had found the perfect woman, and it was clear to everyone that he adored this petite, blonde beauty who gazed back at him in such rapture. He adorned her with clothes, jewelry, and furs made by the top designers in the world. She, in turn, could not believe her good fortune and blossomed under his generous tutelage. She dazzled everyone with her beauty, her down-to-earth charm, and her infectious good nature. Finally, after touring countless countries and attending endless parties, it all came to a screeching halt in Hawaii. Buster collapsed, and Lu found out he had cirrhosis of the liver and would surely die if he continued to drink.

Typical of her take-charge manner in a crisis, Lu quickly assessed the situation and proceeded to arrange for their return home. Upon arriving at the ranch, Lu summoned the house servants and issued her new instructions. "Mister Wharton and I no longer drink any alcoholic beverages. All liquor will be kept under lock and key and is to be served only to our guests. Big Charles and I will retain the keys to the liquor closet and only he and I will disperse the liquor needed for our guests and parties. Anyone caught giving liquor to Mr. Wharton will be fired on the spot." In a softer tone, she added, "I'm sure that won't be necessary. Mr. Wharton says you are all like family, so I know you want what is best for him, too."

In that moment, she won the hearts and loyalty of all the servants, for they did, indeed, love their employer. One of their own ranks had helped raise him, and they knew Miss Mandy would approve of the woman who protected him so fiercely.

Lu approached being the "Lady of the Manor" as she did all things: with determination and a strong desire to learn. She quickly became one of the most renowned hostesses in all of Texas, and famous people from all over the world considered themselves fortunate to sit at her table and enjoy her hospitality.

Buster had little experience with children, and my mother was not overly endowed with maternal instinct, so it was decided that I would live in Vernon with my grandmother and Aunt Avis. I was not at all unhappy about that arrangement because I adored both of them.

My grandmother, known to all as Mama (Maw-Maw), was the epitome of what every grandmother should be—warm, loving, understanding, forgiving, fun, and quick to laugh. She had been raised on a farm in Missouri and married at nineteen to a well-to-do farmer from Texas, who was twenty-five years her senior. She had little education but could read and write, and far more importantly, she had a "gift." When Mama had a premonition, we all listened, especially after she saved my parents from a plane crash. She had never tasted alcohol, never smoked a cigarette, and never learned to drive a car, even though we had a lot of fun trying to teach her as we careened in and out of ditches, laughing so hard we could barely see the road.

Mama was a devout, good-hearted woman who loved her children more than anything in life. This was not lost on Buster, who craved maternal affection. Mama adopted him, and he became a willing addition to her already large brood. He took great delight in surprising her with practical gifts, such as a refrigerator and a commercial-sized freezer that kept her from having to use the cold cellar under the house. Mama was also wise, and she knew Buster had the capacity to love a child; he just needed the opportunity. She began a subtle campaign by taking me to the ranch whenever they were in town. Her efforts were not in vain and in the end, it was Buster who demanded that I come to live with them.

Rita in the arms of her Aunt Avis circa 1945

CHAPTER 5

Passion for Horses

Age Three

On one excursion, Buster took us to the barn to meet his favorite polo pony. After taking one look at Mama Lu, I knew I loved everything about horses—the way they looked, the way they moved, and especially the way they smelled. Staring into her liquid brown eyes, I gently took hold of her jaws and buried my face in her soft muzzle, breathing in the sweet smell of her breath. It smelled like hay mixed with some magical elixir that reached out and touched my soul.

Everything in my short life became eclipsed in that moment, and I knew that I had met a kindred spirit. As I looked at Buster with grateful eyes, he grinned back at me with a look of understanding and said, "*Yee hah*, I think we've got a horse lover on our hands! What do you say, Rita, do you want to ride her?"

I had no words to describe the awe I felt so I just reached up to him and whispered, "Yes, please." As he bent to lift me onto her back, an unspoken bond was forged between Buster and me that could never be broken. Our shared passion for horses was the first bridge that linked us to each other on our journey to becoming father and daughter.

The next week, Buster called my grandmother to ask if she would bring me to the ranch before the weekend because he had a surprise for me and he couldn't wait to give it to me. When we arrived the next day, he was as excited as I was as he loaded us into the hunting wagon and headed to the barn.

As we walked into the paddock area, the first thing I saw was a beautiful paint pony, already saddled and tied to the stall. "He's so little," I breathed.

Buster laughed and said, "He's just your size. He's been waiting for some beautiful little girl like you to come along and take care of him. Would you like that? His name is Duffy, and he's yours if you want him."

My eyes got as big as saucers. "Mine?" I squeaked. As I threw myself into Buster's arms, I said, "I love him, and I'll take the best care of him in the whole world."

From behind me, my grandmother prodded me with a gentle reminder, "What do you say, Rita?" Remembering my manners, I said, "Thank you, Buster. Can I ride him now?"

Buster grinned as he said, "Well, I just happen to have a riding outfit here that I think will fit you, and if your grandmother and Avis don't mind, you and Duffy could take a quick spin to get acquainted."

That quick spin lasted two hours, and I had to be dragged off his back as I protested, "Just a little longer." That ride was my first encounter with ecstasy and I somehow knew that some things cannot be described with words, no matter how eloquent or heartfelt. It is a sacred moment that takes place so deep within the soul that it is known and understood only through the senses. It refuses to be shackled by labels or definitions, and only those with open hearts and minds can recognize and embrace it.

That was only the first of many ecstatic moments that would fill my days at my new home. After all, I now had a pony that needed me, and I couldn't very well live in town if I was going to do a good job caring for him. That was one of many reasons Buster gave to my mother when he suggested I move to the ranch. She resisted for a week or so, saying they traveled a lot, who would take care of me, etc., but it was finally agreed that I would stay with Mama and Avis when Mother and Buster were out of town, and Miss Mandy would take care of me when they were home. Buster said I would love Miss Mandy, and, as always, he was right.

Buster and Rita at a father-daughter horseshow circa 1951

Rita performing in Western competition in 1950

CHAPTER 6

Miss Mandy

Age Three

Miss Mandy was a six-foot-tall Black woman with honey-colored skin and snowy white hair. Even though she was old, she was beautiful and had a regal demeanor. When she smiled, she lit up the room with her white teeth and gold dental work, but when she frowned she could put a grown man to shame, as both her six-foot-five, three-hundred-pound husband and Buster would testify.

Miss Mandy not only ruled our family and the other servants but her power extended past the ranch into town. Once you knew her, you understood why. She had a heart bigger than Texas, and her every waking moment was spent giving little pieces of it to anyone she met. She had helped raise thirty-six children, including Buster, by the time she got to me. Since she could not have children of her own, she opened her arms to any child who needed love, no matter what their color, ethnic background, or creed was. She also played mother hen to the single cowboys who lived in the bunkhouse, and they went to her place for beer and home cooked meals when they were not out on the ranch for extended periods.

Since we lived in the middle of nowhere, beer was hard to come by, especially in a dry county where it was at least thirty miles to the nearest liquor store. So, every week, Miss Mandy either drove to Electra, Texas, or Punkin Center, Oklahoma, to buy several cases of beer. She iced the beer down in a big tin tub and left it outside on a crate under her kitchen window. It was sure handy for everyone to be able to grab a beer and leave a small donation in the kitty jar on the windowsill.

Miss Mandy also kept a close eye on all of the old folks in the flats, although I didn't see how they could get much older than Miss Mandy. When I told her that on one of our missions of mercy, she threw back her head and laughed, saying, "Child, there's old and then there's o-l-d. They be old as dirt."

I adored Miss Mandy and wanted to be with her every waking moment. When she shelled peas or embroidered, I would lay snuggled in her lap and breathe in the rich smell of her. She was comfortable and warm and mostly smelled like cookies and cigarettes. I started smoking at five because I wanted to mimic Miss Mandy when her hands were busy and her cigarette dangled from her mouth and she squinted to keep the smoke out of her eyes. No matter how hard I tried I could never master that trick, so I took up dipping snuff as well. Miss Mandy's husband, Simp, used a sweet, minty snuff, and he taught me how to roll it in my lip. Even after Miss Mandy was not supposed to be my mammy anymore, the three of us shared many wonderful evenings piled up in their big bed watching the television Buster had given them—drinking beer, dipping snuff, and smoking cigarettes.

Life didn't get much better than that, except maybe when I would cook up some mud pies for Buster at the playhouse, or Mandy and I would load up the red wagon with beer, sandwiches, and cigarettes and head to the catfish hole.

Rosie, our cook, almost always caught me stealing cigarettes from the cigarette boxes strategically located around the house and would try to catch me in spite of her five-foot, two-hundred-pound body. "Miss Mandy shouldn't be lettin' you do dat. It just ain't right. I'm gonna tell your Mama. Yes, I am." But no one ever told on Miss Mandy, so poor Rosie would just shuffle back to the kitchen, muttering to herself.

I knew Miss Mandy ruled the roost because of the time Buster stopped us on our way to the catfish hole. With a twinkle in his eye, he lifted up the tea towel covering our contraband in the red wagon and said, "Going fishing, I see." Miss Mandy rocked back on her heels, lifted her head high, and with her most regal look said, "We is. Just like when you was a youngun'." Buster, looking properly chastised, grinned and said, "Well, cigarettes are sure a lot easier to come by than in my day. Y'all bring me some catfish. I haven't had any good catfish in a long time." Miss Mandy smiled at Buster the smile she saved for only her best kids, and the one that we all hoped would be showered on us as often as possible.

Years later, after her husband died and she moved to town, Miss Mandy shocked everyone by taking another husband. My boyfriend Darryl and I loved to go visit her so we could hear the scathingly long list of her new husband's shortcomings. Since Darryl's granddaddy owned liquor stores and Miss Mandy had always been a good customer, he regularly sent her a pint of whiskey on our visits. She would always say the same thing when we arrived: "What sweet children! Thank you. Thank you. Rita, get us some glasses. Darryl, let's move out to the porch where it's cooler. And tell your granddaddy I'm much obliged."

We waited eagerly as she slowly savored the whiskey, licked her lips and said, "Good whiskey." With a soft look at each of us, she said, "Good children." Then, glaring at her poor, oblivious husband rocking quietly at the other end of the porch, she said, "Good for nothing. He sure ain't Simp. Lord, no. No sirree. He don't do nothin' but sit in that rocker, and I mean *nothin'*," she said as her eyes got real wide to make sure we got her meaning.

The first time we got her meaning, we laughed all the way home because Miss Mandy was finally growing a little mean streak, and all because she wasn't getting enough sex.

CHAPTER 7

Polo

Age Three to Four

Buster's world champion polo team, El Ranchito, often hosted polo games at the ranch, and I became enthralled with the long-legged, high-spirited thoroughbreds. My mother and her friends would sigh and say, "There's just something about a man on a polo pony," but I only had eyes for Buster and Mama Lu, his unregistered mare that became a polo legend. Even without authenticating papers, Buster was offered over $150,000 for Mama Lu when he had to retire, but he refused to sell her. She was twenty-five years old then, and she continued to rule the roost until she died at thirty-six.

Cowboys came over just to look at her, saying, "Damn, I never heard of a horse living so long, have you?" Fierce wagers were put on her every time she went down with a stroke, and we would all cheer when she would get up, trot over to a young stud, and kick a slat out of his stall, just to let him know she was back.

As I watched her in her prime, fearlessly charging into a tangle of horses, mallets swinging from every direction as the players jockeyed for the perfect position, I knew I was watching poetry in motion. People say polo is the sport of kings because it's an expensive sport, but more importantly, polo carries an air of royalty because of the valor and majesty that both the horses and the players bring to the field. When the El Ranchito team won the Gibson Trophy in Santa Barbara, the blue bloods were forced to admit that the redneck buckaroos from Texas were champions in every sense of the word, even without pedigrees.

It was common knowledge that Buster's team consisted of employees and neighboring ranchers—predominantly, the Barry brothers—who went on to create a polo dynasty like none other. In describing the Santa Barbara game, the local newspaper had this to say:

> Add the names of these lads to those of Rube Williams and Cecil Smith, as Texans making history in American polo. Bus Wharton's El Ranchito team won every tournament they entered on the coast the past season . . . In Frisco, Bus scored as many goals as the entire opposing team. They downed Cy Bartlett's famed Riviera Four, beat Big Boy William's Hollywood team, trounced Santa Barbara and San Francisco. They hit long, hard, and often, these buckaroos, and played rough! After playing two extra periods in an especially grueling match with the cowboys, the captain of the famous Santa Barbara team took his men off the field. He had had enough! (conceded the game.)

Because I was so small, I was allowed to watch the game from the hood of the car, but I was not allowed to stand up. Some adults had moved into my line of vision and I was trying to decide what to do when, suddenly, a giant shadow fell on me. As I looked up, I saw one of the biggest men I had ever seen, and he was talking to me. "What seems to be the problem, little lady?"

"I can't see," I whispered.

With a sympathetic look, he said, "Hum! Kinda low to the ground, aren't ya? Well, I know how to fix that. Just hop up on my shoulders and I'll take you anywhere you want to go."

When I hesitated, he said, "What's your name, Missy?"

"Rita," I said shyly, holding out my hand.

"Well, now, let me introduce myself properly. My name is John Wayne, but you can call me Uncle Duke. I'm a good friend of Buster's, and I think you and I will be friends, too."

That gentle giant of a man carried me around on his shoulders in one hundred degree heat for the entire game, and by the end of the day, I was his shameless devotee. He and "Big Boy" Williams shared all of Buster's passions—namely wild women, fast horses, fine booze, and good hunting, although I can't say in what order they would have listed them.

Their visits were always bittersweet as they heroically tried to navigate the treacherous terrain of Buster's new domesticity. The past was only discussed when they were alone, and as I grew older, I kept a sharp eye out for those clandestine meetings. They told some real whoppers, but my favorite story was about a party they had thrown at the ranch several years earlier.

They had Neiman Marcus models, showgirls from Vegas, big bands, and great barbeque. The party lasted for three days, and on the fourth day, they woke up naked in a ditch at Four Corners, with a big, buxom blonde laying across them. They had no recollection of how they got there, but they all agreed it was one hell of a party.

I adored those rowdy men, and my love affair with bad boys had begun. Unfortunately, hard living takes its toll, and I grieved as I watched each of them pay the price. Buster was the first to go, "Big Boy" was next, and Uncle Duke was the last to go. The world did not seem nearly as fun or bright when they were gone, but I still like to think of them partying down together, somewhere that has an unlimited supply of all the passions they so loved to indulge together, and no curfew or last call to worry about.

Polo riders colliding

John Wayne (Uncle Duke) vacationing in Hawaii with Rita's parents, 1950

CHAPTER 8

Life with Charles

Age Three to Five

I loved my life at the ranch, but I also looked forward to visiting Charles in Dallas. Since he was a bachelor and always lived in hotels, I knew how to work a hotel by the age of three. If Charles had business to attend, one of his young girlfriends or the bartender would take care of me. I didn't mind a bit because the young girls would play dress-up with me and the bartender would give me a Shirley Temple for dancing on the bar. That pink-cheeked, laughing Irishman gave me my first incentive for learning to dance, and I took both ballet and tap to please him.

Charles was not an early riser, so I would go down to the restaurant to graze from the buffet table and then make my rounds to say good morning to the hotel staff. After putting in an order for coffee and orange juice with room service, I would return to the room and wake Charles up. I loved that morning time with him because that was when he was the most playful; there was always much squealing and giggling as he lifted me high in the air on his feet or held my hands while I jumped on the bed until I was exhausted. After we had our coffee and a shower, we would go the Chateaubriand restaurant where I always ate the same meal: filet mignon (rare), baked potato (butter only), and a hot fudge sundae. Charles was not a big eater so he mostly sat leaning back in his chair as he watched me with an indulgent smile on his face.

"I swear, Buster is turning you into a true carnivore, Princess," he said to me one morning as I devoured my breakfast. "Do you always eat like this?"

"Yes, pretty much," I said after struggling to swallow my food before speaking. When we were through eating, Charles reached across the table and, gazing tenderly into my eyes, took my hands in his. "You know I love you more than anything in the world, and I wish we could spend more time together. You will always be my princess, no matter what. You know that, don't you? Now, let's go to Neiman's and see if we can find you some clothes fit for a princess."

Shopping with Charles was a singular treat because he had exquisite taste and instinctively knew what would look good on any woman. Charles loved women. All women. Years later, when countless women would tell me Charles was the most handsome and charming man they had ever met, I knew exactly what they were talking about. He had a gift. He had a way of making any woman, girl or child, feel like she was the only female in the world. I knew that feeling because he had been charming me since the day I was born, and I felt lucky to be his daughter instead of a brokenhearted wife or girlfriend.

Since I spent most of my time with adults, Charles felt I should see children occasionally. And so he took me to play with some of his friends' children. This particular gang of kids led me away from the house and then ran away laughing, leaving me all alone.

Not being accustomed to a noisy city or the countless houses that loomed over me, I could not get my bearings. As I stood dead still, listening intently as I had been taught, I heard a voice say, "Are you Rita?"

I turned to look at my savior, and there stood the most beautiful boy I had ever seen. He was older than me, at least six or seven, and he was tall and slender with black hair and eyes. He strode toward me with his hand outstretched, and flashing a dazzling smile, he said, "I'm Layton Humphrey Jr. My dad is your dad's best friend and he sent me to find you." Taking my hand in his, he led me back to the house.

My knight had come to rescue me, and that seemed to become an ongoing pattern throughout our lives. As we played that day, he found a red rhinestone ring buried in the dirt. After cleaning the ring, he reached out and put it on my finger. Looking at me intently, and in a solemn voice, he said, "When we grow up, I'm going to marry you, and I will always take care of you."

Though we wisely chose not to marry, he has always kept his promise. Layton became the brother that I was not destined to have within my own family and stood by my side when the rest of the world turned their eyes from the thefts and abuses that would come.

My visits with Charles were always a kaleidoscopic whirl of shopping, restaurants, parties, and colorful people. He did not want me to forget that I was a true Southern lady with impeccable manners, elegant style, and seductive skills in the arts of flirtation and manipulation.

Thus was born the benign rivalry between Charles and Buster that sculpted the woman I would become. Both wanted to create their perfect woman through me, and it did not occur to either of them that their definitions of the ideal woman were in stark contrast to each other, or that I could end up becoming an eccentric blend of Scarlett O'Hara and Annie Oakley. My mother warned them that the average man would not be able to handle such a woman, but for once, they agreed that average men wouldn't be worthy of me, anyway.

Unfortunately, my mother was right. But in their defense, Charles and Buster had only the best of intentions, and I wouldn't change anything that I experienced in my childhood under their loving care and attention.

CHAPTER 9

Ranch Education

Age Three to Five

My life at the ranch provided a very different type of education, but an equally important one. I spent long, glorious days learning to cook, sew, clean, garden, can, and fish with Miss Mandy. She said any self-respecting girl should know how to do all of these things, even if she was rich. Buster agreed that there were necessary skills any Texas woman worth her grit should have, but his agenda was more survival-oriented—riding, swimming, driving, hunting, camping, roping, and subsistence training, which included things like knowing how to change a tire.

Due to my age and size, he decided that swimming was next on my to-learn list, so he taught me the way he had been taught—he threw me into the pool, and said, "Do what comes natural."

As I thrashed wildly in the water trying to make it to the side of the pool, he reached out, took hold of my hand, and pulled me out. "You've got pluck. That's what counts. Form will come later."

I was a busy, happy child and good most of the time, but I did have two exasperating characteristics. The first one was annoying, but not really dangerous: my need to touch everything. Consequently, I was frequently reprimanded for touching things: "Don't touch the fur coat, you'll break the tips; don't touch the puppy, you'll hurt him; don't touch the pretty things, you'll break them; don't touch the toilet seat, you'll catch polio; don't touch me, you'll mess me up." The list of things not to be touched was endless, and for a tactile child, it was pure torture. For me, touch was critical in completing a true evaluation of anything, and I became very proficient at making stealthy contact with something for a brief moment, just long enough to get a sense of it.

My other, more dangerous characteristic was a need to be free and explore. I rarely had a destination when I took off; I just went. I didn't know whether I would end up climbing onto the roof, scaling the magnolia tree, getting lost, or under the wheel of a car. Those were simply unfortunate consequences that, while unpleasant, were still worth the ride.

Buster must have grown tired of looking for me so often, because he finally trained Petey, his Jack Russell terrier, to find me. Petey would sink his sharp little teeth into some part of my clothing and literally drag me home, kicking and screaming. Neither the trouble I got into nor the consequences of some of my impulsive excursions were enough to make me change my ways. In fact, this obsession seemed to grow worse the older I got, and as you might expect, much more dangerous, at least in my parents' opinions.

CHAPTER 10

The Burn

Age Three to Five

Oddly enough, it wasn't any of my adventurous shortcomings that brought about the most traumatic event in my early childhood. It was a cold, rainy day just before Christmas. When Miss Mandy did the family laundry out in the washhouse, I would wash my doll clothes in my miniature duplicate of her old-style washtub with rollers.

On this particular day, I had finished all of my washing and was looking around for something else to do. Miss Mandy saw me eyeing the roller steam press she used to iron sheets, and said, "Oh, no . . . we're not doing that again," referring to the time I got my hand caught between the roller and the press. I sighed and began to look around the room until my eyes fell on the window panes.

The windows were foggy from the heat inside the washhouse, and tiny water rivulets were running down the glass. "Miss Mandy, can I clean the windows?" I asked.

"Yes, you can do that," she answered. "You can use that stepladder over there, but don't get near the heater."

There was a gas heater where Miss Mandy used to boil her starch water, and she had a boiling pot sitting on it. I began to clean the windows, but since the stepladder was so far from the heater, I had to lean way over to get to the windows behind it. As I stood on tiptoe to reach the glass, I lost my balance and fell on top of the heater. The boiling starch water covered the right side of my face and body and I began to scream as it burned into my skin. Miss Mandy ran to me and without a moment's hesitation stripped off my clothes and covered me with a clean towel.

For the first time, her warm body was not a refuge for me: All touch was excruciating agony. Clutching me to her breast, she ran to the house, crying and chanting, "Mandy's sorry, baby. Mandy's sorry. It's going to be okay." She never stopped until she was standing in the upstairs playroom where my parents were entertaining guests. As everyone gathered round, she faced Buster and said, "She burned, Mr. Buster. She burned bad." Looking at her tear-stained face, he patted her shoulder and said, "It'll be all right, Miss Mandy. I'll call the doctor."

By the time Buster got off the phone, my mother had begun her attack on Miss Mandy, screaming, "Where the hell were you? How could you let this happen?" Buster stepped between them and said, quietly, to my mother, "I know you're upset, but this is not the time for that. Let's just worry about Rita right now."

He and Miss Mandy took turns walking me as I screamed and screamed, waiting for a drunk doctor who finally showed up two hours later. He sobered up fast when he saw me, and said, "Bus, I had no idea it was this bad. These are first-degree burns, and the bone is showing on her right shoulder. I'm not qualified for this. You need to get her to Wichita Falls, immediately."

He gave me a shot for the pain and as we headed to the car, I heard my mother saying, "I will not have that woman around my child another minute. She is not going." Buster sighed and whispered to Miss Mandy, "I'm sorry. I'll call you as soon as we know something."

Upon our arrival at the hospital, the burn specialists said I would have to go through a long and painful procedure to remove the starch from my skin and then they could see what could be done to minimize the disfigurement, especially to the right side of my face. They warned that the hair follicles could have been damaged and there could be some loss of sight in the right eye. Mercifully, I have no recollection of the next several days except for those brief periods when I awoke to a world of pain, screaming for Miss Mandy. Buster begged my mother to let him get her, but she hissed, "Over my dead body. That woman will never come near my child again." Pleading with her, he said, "Lu, you're not being reasonable. Let Miss Mandy help her get well and then we'll find someone else. I promise."

They were having their first fight, and as they stood staring defiantly at each other, Buster knew what he had to do. "I'm going to get your mother and Avis. If she can't have Miss Mandy, she needs them here. She barely knows us, Lu." My mother's reaction caught Buster by surprise, and he stepped back as she shot back at him, "Oh, great! They'll have a field day with this. Now they'll have something to prove what a bad mother I am."

Horrified, Buster said, "Lu, this isn't about you. It's about Rita. She's a child and she's in pain and scared. She needs someone to help her get through this. I'm calling them now and I'm sorry if you don't agree with me." As soon as they heard what had happened, Avis said, "Buster, there's no point in you coming to get us; it's just a waste of time. We'll be there in an hour. Oh, and Buster, thanks for calling us."

In a relieved voice, Buster said, "No problem. Thanks for coming," and after a brief silence, added, "I've kinda gotten used to having her around, you know?" Avis heard the catch in his voice and, after a moment, said gently, "I know what you mean."

After six weeks in the hospital, I returned home wrapped up like a mummy from head to toe. I could not go outside, I could not see Miss Mandy, and I could not understand why. My mother explained that Miss Mandy had let me get hurt and therefore could not be entrusted with my care. With the simple logic of a child, I appealed to my mother, saying, "It wasn't her fault. I'm not mad; why are you?" Of course, I was brushed off with clichés: "You're too young to understand; someday, when you're a mother, you'll understand."

With both my freedom and Miss Mandy gone, I grew more frustrated and angry each day. I became a demon child and even resorted to hurting the feelings of one of the servants. When she tried to get me to do something, I screamed, "I don't have to do what you say. You're just an old chocolate drop!" When Buster heard what I had done from a tearful Vera, he was shocked because I had been taught to respect all people, especially the people who worked for us. So when he took me into his office, I knew he was displeased with me. That was a first, and on top of my humiliation, I had no idea what to expect. He spoke to me quietly, explaining how Vera felt. He talked to me about respect, about all I had been through, and I found myself feeling less angry and better about myself. I could not believe how different he was from my mother in the way he handled discipline and punishment. His way was focused on learning through understanding and compassion rather than intimidation and rage. He only deviated from that style once, when he caught me smoking in my mother's dressing room using one of her cigarette holders. He spanked me with my mother's hairbrush but later explained that he was scared because I could have caught the house on fire when I threw the cigarette into the trash full of tissues.

Even at that age, I knew the awful fear of fire when you live in the middle of nowhere.

After Buster had finished speaking, I whispered, "What can I do to make it right?" He smiled and said, "Just go apologize to Vera. She'll appreciate that. And give her one of your great hugs."

I climbed off the couch and walked over to him. "Thank you, Buster," I said, shyly reaching up to hug him. After we hugged, he said, "How would you feel about calling me Daddy Buster? Now, only if you want to, of course." I smiled and replied, "I would like that, Daddy Buster." Looking relieved, he said, "Well, I'm glad that's settled. Now let's go find Vera." Buster had just had his first taste of the unconditional love of a child, and he liked it.

CHAPTER 11

Home for Good

Age Four to Five

Within six months life was back to normal for me, at least physically. There was minimal scarring except for on my right shoulder and a large red area on my neck. My hair grew back quickly, thicker than ever, and I was ready to move on with my life except for one thing. The emotional scar I carried in my heart was far worse than the physical scarring. Having Miss Mandy taken from me at such a critical time and in such an abrupt manner was to be my first memorable lesson in loss. I had no way of knowing that it was just the first of many and that I would become a master at that dubious art. One good thing had come out of it, and that was the bonding taking place between Daddy Buster and me. Since I wasn't allowed to be with Miss Mandy, I spent most of my time with him and occasionally we would sneak over to her house while we were supposed to be out riding. We would hide the horses among the pecan trees near the greenhouse and creep in through Miss Mandy's back door. It always seemed like she had just cooked one of my favorite desserts—chocolate cake, chocolate cream pie, pecan pie, or peach cobbler. When I said how lucky that was for me, she and Daddy Buster would smile at each other and with a twinkle in their eyes, say, "Yes, you are a lucky girl."

As we ate our treats, Miss Mandy would ask me questions about what I was learning and she would always end up rolling her eyes and saying, "Mr. Buster, do you realize that this a girl child? She look like a boy most of the time, riding 'roun' here like a wild Indian." Daddy Buster grinned sheepishly and said, "I know, but she likes it and she's good at it."

"Well, that may be," Miss Mandy argued, "but she's still got to learn girl things too.

What man is gonna want a girl that can't cook or sew or take care of a house? Besides, it ain't natural for a girl to best a boy; he won't like it." Daddy Buster nodded and promised he would give it some thought.

When he casually brought up the subject of a nanny with my mother, she told him she had been looking for someone with the right credentials and that she would check with their friend to see if they could recommend someone temporarily. Some well-meaning person gave her the name of a woman who came to personify the word *fear* for me. She was a very stern and very white woman, which led me to nickname her the Ghost Lady. When she looked at me, I could see her nose wrinkle as if she had smelled something bad, and if I tried to touch her, she would say, "I don't believe in coddling children." I could tell she thought I had gotten way too much of that already.

My parents had to go to Fort Worth for a couple of days and they thought it would be a good opportunity to find out if my new nanny could handle me alone. The first day went fine, but things really went south the evening of the second day. I had taken my bath and was in my pajamas but decided to take a quick run down the hill on my bike. I loved that wild ride, going as fast as I could until I rattled over the cattle guard at the bottom of the hill. I returned to the house, flushed and happy, because I was beginning to feel like my old self again. Ghost Lady was standing at the front door with her arms folded across her chest.

Her very white face had turned almost purple as she reached out and slapped me, screaming, "Where have you been? I've been looking everywhere for you." I was in total shock because no one had ever hit me in the face before. The right side of my face was still sensitive from the burns, and pain spread throughout my body like a wildfire, reminding me of that awful night. She grabbed me by the arm, but I yanked away from her and ran to the kitchen, throwing myself against Rosie's body. Rosie was our short, rotund cook and I knew she would protect me from Ghost Lady. Breathing heavily, she glared at Rosie and said, "Let go of that child; she has disobeyed me and must be punished."

Rosie flashed her million-dollar smile and said, "What'd she do, Ms. Black? I know she can be a handful."

Ghost Lady recounted my dastardly deed and Rosie chuckled, saying, "She's kind of a free spirit, but that's just her way. She don't mean no harm by it. The good Lord makes us the way we is."

Ms. Black grabbed my arm, jerking me to her and hissed, "I don't need no nigger to tell me how to do my job!"

As she dragged me from the kitchen into the new washroom, Rosie ran behind us crying, "Ms. Black, you can't do this. Mr. Buster'll have a fit. He love dis chil'. Please don't do this. Lord, Lord. Jesus, help us . . . "

Ghost Lady pulled me into the washroom, slammed the door, and looked around the room. Spotting a telephone cord, she wound it into a short whip and began beating me with it, screaming, "You'd better mind me. You will mind me!"

I could hear Rosie yelling for her husband, Big Charles, and I hung onto her voice like a lifeline. Suddenly, the door flew open and Big Charles stood like a towering inferno glaring at the crazy Ghost Lady. He ripped the cord from her hand and in a deadly quiet voice said, "Would you like to try using this on me?" She stared at his six-foot-five, 350-pound physique and grew even whiter. She took a step back. "I didn't think so," he said with a look of disdain. He reached down to pick me up and his eyes burned into her as he said quietly, "Don't ever touch her again."

We went into the kitchen where Rosie stripped off my clothes, clucking over the many ugly red welts on my small body. Her eyes welled with tears as she held me close and crooned, "I'm sorry, chil'. I'm sorry I'm jus' an old woman that no bad white folks gots to listen to. I'm sorry I couldn't keep you safe." Turning to Big Charles, she said, "I think we better take her into town to Ms. Judd's. She'll be safe there, and they'll know what to do."

I begged Rosie not to tell my grandmother what had happened because I was afraid Daddy Buster would think I was too much trouble, and I knew my mother thought I needed some discipline. She reluctantly agreed, at least until my parents got home, so she told Mama and Avis that she did not think the new nanny was going to work out and that it would be best if I stayed there until my parents returned. They were thrilled to have me, as always, and did not question their good fortune until Avis gave me a bath the next day. She gasped when she saw the welts and bruises on my body and asked me what happened. I lied. I told her I fell on my bike. She did not buy that for a minute and, looking at me sternly, said, "Rita, these marks were not caused by a bike accident. I want to know who did this to you, now."

I tearfully told her what had happened and begged her not to tell Mother and Daddy Buster. "Why ever not?" she asked. Looking at her with solemn brown eyes, I whispered, "They'll think I'm too much trouble and they won't want me anymore."

My aunt jumped to her feet and yelled for my grandmother. Mama came running into the bathroom and stopped in horror as her eyes fell on my naked body. Avis's voice, hard as stone, said, "The new nanny did that. I'm calling Lula."

My parents had just walked in the door at the ranch, so my mother was not thrilled with having to deal with yet another Rita crisis. Avis described the vivid marks on my body, growing more hysterical by the moment. Finally, my mother responded, saying, "Avis, I'm sure you're overreacting. Rita could use a little discipline. All of you spoil her rotten."

Avis keened like a woman in mourning, and yelled, "Rita knew you would say that. She was savagely beaten! Don't you care?"

Rosie had just informed Daddy Buster about what had happened and he strode into the room, taking the phone from my mother. "Avis, how is she?"

Avis took a deep, quivering breath and said, "She'll be fine. She's more afraid that you won't want her anymore."

After a long silence, in a ragged voice, Daddy Buster said, "I promise you, that woman will be gone within the hour. And, Avis, if you and Mama will allow it, I'd like to come get Rita. I want her home now."

Hope lit my aunt's voice as she asked, "Are you sure, Buster?"

"I've never been more sure of anything in my life. Tell her I'm on my way."

When I saw him standing at the front door with tears in his eyes, I knew I was going home for good. He said, "Hey, little squirrel," as he bent to pick me up.

"Hi, Daddy," I said as I wrapped my arms around his neck.

Big Charles (*far left*) with Mrs. E. Paul Waggoner, Electra Waggoner Biggs, E. Paul Waggoner, and Johnny Biggs

Aunt Avis in a cotton field

CHAPTER 12

Learning to Drive

Age Five

Some women are not meant to have children, and my mother was one of them. I think any doubts she may have had about that fact were quickly alleviated during her pregnancy. She had suffered some of the worst possible side effects: morning sickness that lasted seven months, milk fever, and phlebitis. I am quite sure none of those unpleasant conditions helped to endear me to my mother. In her opinion, the loss of her figure alone was sufficient reason to abhor pregnancy. Nevertheless, she loved me in her own way and therefore she tackled motherhood in her usual indomitable style.

Because she wanted only the best for me, she concluded that I needed a surrogate mother like Miss Mandy had been, but with better credentials. That was a tall order but she was on a mission now, and we all suspected I would have a new nanny very soon.

Meanwhile, Daddy was teaching me how to shoot and drive a car. He had ordered a custom-made, child-sized rifle and shotgun for me, and we were going duck hunting. He took me to the tank just north of Prairie Dog Town because it had a good duck blind and was close to the house, in case I went "girlie" on him. We settled into the blind and waited. It was cold and damp but I would have chewed my arm off before complaining.

Finally, Daddy said, "Here they come. Since this is your first time, I think it would still be sporting if you let them land on the water. Now, remember what I told you: Pick your bird, aim carefully with both eyes open, and squeeze the trigger." I did exactly as he said, except for one small detail. The rifle just happened to be resting on my index finger on top of the blind, and when the gun fired, the recoil hammered my finger into the wood. I yelped as pain shot through my finger, but Daddy was shouting, "You got him! Your very first try and you got him!"

He sent Tar Baby, his black lab, to get the duck and turned to hug me. I was smiling as tears rolled down my face. He saw the tears, became alarmed, and asked, "What's wrong?"

I held up my finger and he gently took hold of it. Giving a low whistle, he said, "Looks like you might lose that nail, but I bet you won't ever rest a gun barrel on your finger again. What a girl! You got your first duck and your first hunter's wound on your first time out. Wait till your mother hears about this."

My mother was a competitive woman so she was proud of my achievement, but Daddy was also teaching her how to shoot and after the third telling of the story during dinner, she'd had enough. I, on the other hand, was feeling very full of myself as I basked in his praise and tried not to think of how the dead birds had looked and smelled. I adored my new daddy and I would do anything he loved to do, no matter how distasteful.

Luckily, driving did not present any repugnant challenges, and I especially loved the feeling of freedom it gave me. Daddy had bought me a pale yellow convertible that ran on foot pedal power, and I navigated all of the interconnecting sidewalks between the house, the barn, and the shop area.

The first Christmas that my stepbrother, Bucky, spent with us, Daddy gave us a small red car with a lawn mower engine that went one mile an hour. We quickly decided that was way too slow, so not long after, he bought us a small, pale yellow Model A Ford with a surrey top. That car went thirty-five miles an hour and we were in high cotton. After that came the Green Goose—a full-sized, chartreuse green, Model T Ford body with a striped and fringed surrey top. It went fifty-five miles per hour, and since there were no doors, you really had to hold on tight. And just to make things interesting, Daddy had installed a "moo-horn" and an electric shock in the back seat. We would load the Green Goose full of kids and tear around the barn, sounding the moo-horn and pressing the shock button occasionally to see who would jump. The poor hunting dogs and every other living creature in the area would go crazy, creating a discordant symphony of sounds.

Daddy was determined that I would not be a fearful driver, and by the age of twelve, I was driving him to see Dick Jones in Electra. He would snooze on the way home and occasionally ask, "How fast you going?"

"Just a little over eighty," I would answer.

"Well, know your limits; don't drive any faster than you think you can handle. Keep it on the road." For someone who rarely drove under one hundred miles per hour on the highways, he thought any speed under that was reasonable.

I never minded taking Daddy to Dick Jones's because there was always something interesting in the backyard of the liquor store. Once, it was an alligator, and another time it was a javelina pig. Dick and Daddy tried to convince me the pig was a warthog from Africa. Dick really knew how to tell a tall tale, and I would sit transfixed for hours, listening to his stories.

Rumor had it that Dick had run with Pretty Boy Floyd, and when the Feds were closing in, Pretty Boy gave him the remaining money and said, "They don't want you. Take the money and make a decent life for yourself." Later, Pretty Boy was killed in a blazing gunfight, but Dick was in Electra courting his future wife. She was from a well-to-do family who were not exactly thrilled about their daughter dating an alleged gangster. Ever resourceful, Dick built an airplane, stole her from under their noses, and flew off into the wild blue yonder. After their honeymoon, he called her family with the good news and said he would be happy to bring her back if they would accept him. They begrudgingly agreed, so Dick promptly returned to Electra and opened up a liquor store with Pretty Boy's money. The rest is history, and who would have dreamed that my first love would be the grandson of that blessed union?

Years later, after the death of his beloved wife, Dick was living in a rest home and I received a frantic phone call from his grandson Darryl. The director had called to say that Dick would have to leave because he was breaking the rules. When I asked what rule he was breaking, Darryl chuckled and said, "He's visiting the ladies' rooms at night."

I laughed and said, "Well, good for him. So what's the problem? Are the ladies complaining?"

Darryl said, "Oh, no. They love him. It's a rules thing, I guess. What should I do?"

"Just tell the director he should be grateful Dick is performing an invaluable service by making a lot of little old ladies very happy. Heck, they should be paying Dick, but tell the director that you'll pay an extra hundred a month for any inconvenience he may have caused."

The director agreed, out of the goodness of his heart, of course, and Dick was allowed to continue his good deeds until he died.

Rita and her stepbrother, Bucky, riding in her new toy car outfitted with a lawn mower engine

CHAPTER 13

The Strange Men

Age Four to Five

At the end of a hot, lazy summer, just before I turned five, an event occurred that would change all of our lives, especially mine. My parents were at Lake Kemp, just twelve miles down the road from our ranch, and my brother and I had been left in the care of Rosie and Big Charles.

We had just finished dinner, and while Rosie cleaned up the kitchen, Big Charles was outside cleaning the grill. I heard voices and started toward the door but Rosie put her finger to her lips and shook her head, "No." She had heard the unfamiliar voices, too, and walked quietly to the door to peek out. She stood very still for a moment and then, whirling, grabbed me by the hand and picked up my little brother. Her eyes were wide and stern. She did not say a word, but instead, pursed her lips shut and shook her head vehemently. She crept into the dining room, through the living room, and out the back door.

Sensing something was wrong, Bucky began to whimper, but Rosie hissed, "Shhhh!" and he remained quiet as we crept through the dark. We passed the bird aviaries on the north corner of the house, the fish pond in the front, the aviaries on the south corner, and did not stop until we reached the root cellar on the south side. It was a large, cool space under the house where Rosie kept all of our canned harvest from the summer. The entrance was a heavy storm door that opened up into steep stairs leading underground. I knew that I could not lift that door because I had tried many times, so I was relieved when Rosie lifted it easily.

Gesturing for me to go first, she quietly lowered the door and followed me down into the darkness. She did not turn on the light, but after fumbling in the dark for a minute, she struck a match and looked around. Pulling us close to her, she began to whisper fierce instructions, mostly looking at me: "There are some bad men here, and Big Charles is protecting us. I have to go back so you have to be a big girl and take care of your brother. You stay put, no matter what you hear, until I come's back to get ya."

As Bucky began to whimper again, she kissed his cheek and whispered, "We're going to play hide-and-seek, sweetheart. And you can't make a sound or you'll lose. Rita, remember what I said. I'll be back as fast as I can." Rosie then hid us behind some large burlap bags and hurried up the stairs and out into the night.

The same instinct that keeps animal babies quiet and in their den when their mother goes for food kept us silent for the longest time. The only sound we made was the soft whisper of our own breathing. The air felt cold and damp as we sat huddled in the dark, wondering what was happening above us.

As it turned out, Big Charles had his hands full. A short time earlier, as he was cleaning the grill, two men in dark suits quietly approached him from behind. As he turned, expecting to see familiar faces, one of the men stepped up close to him and asked if Buster was home.

Big Charles sized up the situation quickly and realized these men were not friends. He told the man my parents were out of town and would not return for a week. The man doing all the talking then pulled a gun and pointed it at Big Charles's forehead, grinned and said, "You strike me as being a smart nigger. Are you? Would you die for some whitey that don't give a damn about you? Just tell me the truth, and we'll get on with our business. We don't have no business with you unless we have to."

Big Charles wisely decided to "play dumb". "I is smart, and I sho don't wanna die for no white man. I swear, boss, I's telling the truth."

Staring hard at Big Charles, the man said, "What about the children? Aren't there two kids?"

"Yes, sir. Two young-uns. But they done took 'um with 'em."

The man stared at Big Charles a moment longer, and then, laughing, turned to his partner and said, "He's telling the truth. Ain't no nigger gonna risk his life for a white man. Let's get out of here."

The two men disappeared as quietly as they had come. Rosie flew out the door and into her husband's arms. Looking up at him with tears streaming down her face, she said, "I never been so proud in all my born days." Rosie and Big Charles gripped each other's shaking hands. Charles asked, "Where are the children?"

"They's in the root cellar. Scared to death, I 'spect. Let's go get 'em."

After retrieving us from the root cellar, Big Charles called Shorty and Jessie, our two top hands, and asked them to get some armed men up to the house and to send someone to get my parents. While we waited, Rosie fixed everyone homemade peach ice cream and as we all sat around the warm kitchen, laughing and talking, it seemed like a party. Bucky and I forgot about the bad men.

When my parents arrived and I saw the stricken look on their faces, I knew life would never be the same for any of us. After my parents held us like they would never let go, Daddy turned to Big Charles and, his eyes brimming with tears, he held out his hand and said, "How can I ever thank you? I honestly don't know if I would have been brave enough to do what you did. I'm much obliged."

Big Charles smiled through his tears and, grasping Daddy's hand in both of his huge hands, said, "I don't need no thanks. You would've done the same for me. I love these children, and I was proud to protect 'em."

After a quiet moment between them, Daddy turned to Rosie, who had been hugging my mother, and scooped her up in his arms, which was no small feat, saying, "And let's not forget about our other hero." Rosie giggled and shushed him, as she weakly insisted he put her down. Gently setting her back on the ground, he said, "So, Rosie, are we having a celebration or not? Where's my peach ice cream?"

"Lordy, no. I ain't doing no celebratin' till we figure out a way to get help if we need it," Rosie said as she handed him a bowl of ice cream.

Living twelve miles from town, we knew we could not depend on the police, so an emergency siren was installed on our house. You could hear that thing for miles; we knew because someone was always accidentally setting it off. Luckily, we never had to use it for an emergency of that sort again, but it was a great catalyst for anyone to retell the story about Big Charles and the bad men. Everyone speculated about who would have ordered such a thing, but we never knew who sent those men.

The only bad thing to come out of the whole ordeal was the loss of even more of my freedom. I could not spend the night at my friends' homes, and I could not go anywhere alone, even on the ranch. That meant that if I wanted to ride, one of the cowboys had to be available to go with me. I tried sneaking off by myself, but after the time I brought some tourists back to the house, my parents lost all patience. Daddy asked me why I had done such a foolish thing, and I told him I was just being neighborly. "They were Yankees and had never seen a ranch before so I was taking them for a little tour."

Trying not to smile, Daddy said as sternly as he could, "Well, you're gonna have to be a little less neighborly or you're gonna scare your mother to death. She's still not over that incident with the bad guys and she's afraid you don't understand that there are bad people in the world who would hurt you. You do know that now, don't you, Deets?" He called me Deets sometimes.

I nodded solemnly because I had learned that lesson on that awful night. For better or worse, I now knew there are bad people in the world who would kill you just because you are rich and famous. Nevertheless, it went against my nature to hate or fear people, so I continued to welcome all strangers, but the seeds of reclusion had been planted deeply in my subconscious.

That became more and more apparent as I grew older and consistently sought out secluded homes. City people could never see the logic in my idea of security because they believe there is safety in numbers and lights and have come to fear the lonely places in the world. My grandmother said city people couldn't hear Nature talking to them anymore because there was too much concrete between them and the earth. I, on the other hand, felt safe in the lonely places because by day, I could see my enemy coming and make a stand of my own choosing, and at night I could depend on the animals warning me if there was danger. But best of all, I could see the open skies and stars and I could hear God speak to me through His creatures and soft breezes rustling through the trees.

CHAPTER 14

Cinco de Mayo

Age Five

On a large ranch with hundreds of people there is a tragedy of some kind almost every day. They can range from the death of a newborn chick to the death of someone you know and love. Consequently, ranch life teaches you to bury your dead and move on, because animals still need to be fed and crops still need to be planted. Ranchers and farmers do not have the luxury of self-pity, so it seemed perfectly natural for me to shift my attention from the burn and the bad men to something exciting that would happen very soon.

I was starting kindergarten, and I could not wait to learn to read. Daddy had been sharing his favorite books with me every night. I looked forward to hearing more about Black Beauty, Old Yeller, or the yearling. They were all very real to me and I knew I wouldn't feel so lonely when my parents were gone if I could read about my new friends. Kindergarten would also provide me with something I did not know I had longed for—other kids. I seldom played with other children, and it did not take me long to realize I was going to have to make some adjustments. I really wanted to be with the girls but the things they liked to do bored me to tears. My new friend Pam could spend hours dressing and undressing her doll, which I thought was the stupidest thing I had ever seen, but I was determined to get along. As we "played dolls" I would gaze longingly at the bright red dump truck and the yellow, big-bladed Caterpillar the boys were using over in the sand pile. If Pam caught me looking at them, she would say, "Don't look at them. They're just nasty ol' boys."

Nevertheless, I envied those boys moving the dirt around and getting dirty while they did it. I was sent to school in a very presentable fashion but by noon I had either soiled or torn the dress I was made to wear. Within a month I hardly owned a dress that hadn't had the skirt torn off from bailing out of the swing. In contrast, Pam arrived at school looking like a porcelain doll and went home looking the same way. She was an amazement to me and I felt lucky to have such a sophisticated friend.

I loved kindergarten and learned to read quickly, adding a new friend to my book menagerie named Babar the elephant. But on my birthday in November, all of my animal friends got some very stiff competition. Daddy gave me my very own polo pony named Cinco de Mayo, which means "Fifth of May" in Spanish. He was a sorrel gelding that Daddy thought would do well in dressage, and our training began immediately.

Cinco's training was going better than mine, as I was used to a Western saddle with a saddle horn up front. An English saddle does not have one. Every time we came to an abrupt stop, I would slide over the saddle, down his neck and to the ground. He could have trampled me but instead, he would stop short and look at me, nose to nose, with a look of patient disdain.

My trainer, Billy Mayer, would yell, "Get back on. Try again." Daddy would not let my mother watch during those first lessons because he knew she would insist I quit. And even though I took a lot of falls the first few weeks, my pride was more injured than my body, and I was determined to be ready for the Father-Daughter dressage competition in a couple of months. After one especially humiliating day, Daddy found me sulking in my room and asked what was wrong. Sighing, I mumbled, "I just can't do it. Do you think it's because I'm a girl?"

Horrified, Daddy took my hands in his and stared hard into my eyes. He said, "I don't ever want to hear you say that again. You can do anything you want to do, if you want it badly enough, even if you are a girl. Don't ever let anyone ever tell you any different. Just keep working at it. You'll get the hang of it."

That was a pivotal moment for me because my self-concept as a strong, capable girl was etched into my soul. Taking Daddy's words to heart, I worked with Cinco hard every day and it began to pay off in a lot of blue ribbons. I rode in many competitions that year, both Western and English, and even though I won a lot, I never loved anything more than those father-daughter shows, even if we came in dead last. It's not always about winning. Sometimes it's just about enjoying the ride.

CHAPTER 15

Flying Solo

Age Five

In the spring, Mother and Daddy took the polo team to Hawaii for the summer. Uncle Duke (John Wayne) was there and I knew Daddy was looking forward to spending time with him. Mother was looking forward to the polo matches and parties. I moved into town with Mama and Avis where I always loved to be, so it wasn't so bad. Even though I really liked kindergarten, I was ready for the summer so I could get back to all of my usual activities at the ranch.

Finally, the school year was over and I eagerly awaited my graduation. Since my parents could not be there, Avis came with scotch tape all over her face after having several moles removed that day. She looked funny but I could always count on her to be there, no matter how inconvenient or embarrassing. As it turned out, I had something even more wonderful to do this summer. Daddy called to say that the horses were missing me so much that they had asked him to bring me to Hawaii.

I was ecstatic but I grew quiet as I heard a serious tone creep into his voice. "There's just one hitch, Deets," he said. "You'll have to fly here by yourself. Do you think you could do that?"

"How far is it?" I asked.

"It's a long way, honey, and it will take a long time," he replied.

After thinking for a minute, I asked, "Can I take my Babar books with me?"

Daddy laughed and said, "You can bring anything you want . . . except Cinco, of course."

I giggled and said, "Okay, Daddy. I love you," and handed the phone to Avis so they could plan my trip.

Mama and Avis were not nearly as thrilled as I was about me flying cross-country and over the ocean by myself, but they agreed to put me on the plane. The airline arranged for specific stewardesses to hand me off to the next stewardess throughout my journey, and I remember them being very kind. But of course, my real support was tucked inside a miniature set of Babar books that I clutched to my body, even when I slept. I reassured my elephant friends whenever they needed it, telling them they were very brave and that I was proud of them. When we finally arrived and I walked out onto the top platform of the plane's steps, I was amazed to see a crowd of people waving up at me. I squinted into the sun and saw my parents hurrying up the steps toward me. As we hugged and kissed, there were bulbs flashing everywhere as men took pictures of us and shouted out questions to me.

"How was your trip? Were you scared? Were they nice to you?" I couldn't imagine what all the excitement was about but I was proud to be there, so I told them, "My flight was great. I wasn't scared. They were very nice to me," which seemed to make a lot of people happy.

It turned out that I was the youngest child to cross the Pacific Ocean by myself, and the airline used the moment to advertise the safety of flight to a still somewhat leery nation. Beautiful young girls in grass skirts draped gardenia leis around my neck, and I was captivated by the exotic smells and the rhythmic beating of the drums. From that moment forward, the gardenia became my favorite flower and I could never smell that fragrance without thinking of Hawaii. I took it all in because I wanted to share every detail with Mama. She was always talking about Heaven and I couldn't wait to tell her that I had found paradise here on earth. It was a long way from Texas but it was worth the trip.

CHAPTER 16

Hawaiian Grace

Age Five to Six

My parents had leased a beautiful Oriental-style house on Diamond Head and the views of the ocean were breathtaking. Having never seen the ocean, I became an instant devotee and spent every waking moment there. I had discovered a new world and dear Grace became my guide. She was a young Hawaiian woman, part Japanese, who worked in our house.

Grace and I had a natural affinity for one another, so my parents left me in her care more often than not. She was the gentlest soul I had ever met and seemed to delight in all things, especially nature. She laughed easily and often, yet was equally quick to tear up. She was a Buddhist and respected all life, no matter how small or seemingly insignificant. She did not speak much about her religion, but as I came to know her, I realized we knew the same God even though she called him something different. And I would wonder how big God must be to live here with Grace as well as in Texas with Mama and Miss Mandy.

I liked the idea of having a Big God and I was especially fascinated by his many faces. I was beginning to see that God looked and acted differently, depending on where you were. In Texas, God looked rugged and could be somewhat unforgiving, but in Hawaii, he was all sparkling sands, aquamarine water, and lush green hills. And from everything Grace told me about the Buddha, I knew he and Jesus must be good buddies. I liked this new Buddhist face of God and I found Grace to be the perfect teacher on this new journey. As we walked the beach barefoot, she pointed out the most minute sea creatures, the curve and sound of a seashell, the warmth of the sand on our feet and the light dancing off the waves. I loved seeing God through her eyes; it was like opening up another wondrous chapter in a magnificent book.

I knew that Mother and Daddy were being very generous in sharing Grace with me because she was a woman of many talents. She was not only a trained masseuse but was also a highly skilled chef. She could create exquisite floral centerpieces by carving ordinary fruits and vegetables. She was a real treasure and we all knew it, but for Grace and me, every day was an adventure as we grazed our way from raw fish on the beach to roasted pig at a luau.

Grace encouraged me to take hula lessons, and I began studying with one of the legendary hula dancers in Hawaii. She taught me the dance "Lovely Hula Hands," which tells a beautiful story, as all hulas do, and I very much liked the idea of storytelling by hand. However, had I known that I would be made to do that dance, in a grass skirt, on the stage in the auditorium in front of my first-grade class, I think I might have foregone the hula lessons. I am pretty sure that is the night my dislike of being in front of a large group began.

My mother found a brilliant pastel portrait artist and we both had our portraits done, but Daddy declined. I was not thrilled with having to sit perfectly still for an hour each day, but I knew my real dad, Charles, would be ecstatic when he heard. He thought every proper young lady should have her portrait painted so that when she grew old, she could remember how beautiful she had been. Daddy Buster said that Daddy Charles was a romantic, but I just smiled because I knew they were both romantics in different ways. That was one of the things I loved most about them.

Mother was so pleased with the portraits that she commissioned the artist to do one of my brother, Bucky, who was not with us. I was so glad she thought of that because, years later, after his children were born, Buck seemed thrilled when I gave it to him.

Mother and Daddy were definitely enjoying the polo season and the parties, but I wasn't so sure about Uncle Duke. His wife, Chata, a fiery beauty, was displaying signs of jealousy and throwing temper tantrums. Late one night, Uncle Duke woke the entire household to find out if she had called or come by. They had quarreled, she had taken off, and he could not find her anywhere. As I peeked into the living room, I saw Uncle Duke sitting on the couch, holding his head in his hands and crying. "I know she's a ring-tailed tooter, but God, I love her. You have to help me find her, Bus."

My parents went with him, of course, but the next day when my mother said she wished Uncle Duke could find a less combustible wife, Daddy laughed and said it would never happen. “He likes ’em fiery. Did you see how they made up when we found her? He’s gotta have the passion.”

After giving the whole matter some thought, I was still most taken with the notion of seeing a grown man cry, especially a man as big as Uncle Duke. And over a woman, no less.

CHAPTER 17

Grace at the Ranch

Age Five to Six

As all good things must, our summer came to an end and I began to dread leaving Grace. Then, she told me she was coming home with us and although I was elated, I was having a hard time picturing her in Texas. Once we arrived at the ranch, I could see Grace was beginning to have a few doubts herself. Her eyes wide with shock, she gazed out over the endless expanse of red dirt and mesquite trees that surrounded our lush oasis on the hill.

Taking her hand, I said, "It's not as bad as it looks. I'll show you the good things like you did for me in Hawaii. Don't be afraid. I'm here with you." Smiling through her tears, she hugged me and said, "That is more than enough."

Grace tried very hard to adjust to our way of life, but I often found her crying in her room, especially on rainy days. I was amazed to see her cry so openly, because I had been raised to believe that big girls don't cry. When I asked her about it, she said crying was a very good thing because it released emotions and rids the body of toxins. That sounded okay to me, and I couldn't wait to tell the cowboys because they never cried. I had watched them sew up cuts on their own fingers and they never shed a tear. Cowboys were tough but they were smart too, like an animal is smart; they just seem to know things. Miss Mandy said it was because they spent so much time alone on the range and they got to listen to God a lot more than most folks. That made sense to me and I was betting they would understand Grace's ways, although I couldn't see any of them tuning up for a good cry.

As it turned out, I needn't have worried because everyone loved her as much as I did. No matter how different she was in appearance, culture, and religion, it was easy to spot her kind heart, and that made her one of us. That was lucky for me because when Mother and Daddy left on safari, Grace and I went to a barbeque or a fish fry almost every weekend. While the grown-ups played poker, the children ran around the yard and through the house like a pack of wild dogs, slyly stealing sips of beer from the seemingly distracted poker players. However, once the dancing started, the children began to drop in their tracks like exhausted puppies, exactly as the adults had known they would. It's amazing what a good sedative a few sips of beer can be, and in those days it wasn't considered child abuse.

Grace adapted to our ways as much as possible, and she was a sight for sore eyes in her Western outfit at her first rodeo. She never got the hang of horses, though, which really surprised me. Daddy said it was because she got a bad taste in her mouth about horses when our palomino, Goldie, dragged her around the paddock that time. I said, "Yeah, but that was just her first try. You gotta get back on." Daddy chuckled and said, "Well, not everybody loves horses the way we do, and maybe getting drug by her ankle wasn't much fun for her." I shook my head and asked, "Have you ever seen that happen before, Daddy?" He put on his serious face and said, "No, I can't say as I have, except maybe in rodeos."

One of the cowboys, Eddie Browder, had taken a real shine to Grace and he didn't care if she liked horses or not. He had sandy red hair and a ruddy complexion that had no business being in the Texas sun. When he wasn't cowboying, he looked like his mother had scrubbed him with a toothbrush, all duded up in his crisp white shirt, pressed denim jeans, his hair slicked back and smelling good. It seemed to me every cowboy in the world must use Old Spice. When he came around looking like that, I knew he had come a-courting. Grace was still grieving for her lost love, an American pilot killed in the war, but she could see what a good man Eddie was and welcomed his friendship. For two quiet people, they sure laughed a lot and we all thought they might end up a couple, but that was not meant to be. After about a year, Grace told me that as much as she loved me and everyone else on the ranch, she was homesick for her home and her people. I could understand that, so I told her I knew she had to go but I was glad for the time we'd had. She hugged me and said, "It's raining. Let's go for a walk." I have never taken a walk in the rain since without thinking of her.

Grace Rosen, Rita's nanny from Hawaii, sitting on poof in front of the aquarium at the ranch

CHAPTER 18

An Eccentric Home

Age Six

I missed Grace a lot when she left us but I was a busy child with a full schedule, so I did not have time to get too desolate. I was in second grade and taking piano, tap, and ballet lessons, not to mention my Blue Bird group. I also had to make time for riding, hunting, skiing, and swimming, depending on the season.

I was very excited about the dance lessons because I couldn't wait to impress my friend, Joe the bartender, with everything I was learning. I was betting he would give me two Shirley Temples the next time I danced on his bar. I liked the piano lessons, too, but I did not like having to practice an hour every day.

When I really missed Grace, what helped the most were my new friends. I had always had a lot of grown-up friends but I'd only had one friend my age, and I did not get to see Layton very often. Thanks to Grace, I had a lot of new friends now. I knew almost all of the children at the ranch headquarters and we often rode our horses or our bikes together. I also had my friends in town, and occasionally one of my girlfriends spent the night with me, but if the truth be known, I don't think any of them enjoyed coming to my house. They were afraid of all the stuffed animals, the bear rugs, the guns, and even the dining room table and chairs that were covered in leather and calf skin. I thought it was just another "girl thing" that I didn't get, but I later realized that a lot of people would find our lifestyle strange if not distasteful. Since it was all I had ever known, I thought nothing of the eccentricities of our home. To me, it was a large, comfortable ranch house with the usual accouterments of a gun collection, animal trophies, Native American artifacts, Remington sketches, and the uncharacteristic touch of an exquisite art collection from around the world. My grandmother Electra and my father were avid collectors, and our home reflected just how far and wide they had traveled.

Other unusual features of our house were the glass bird aviaries, the exotic pets, the oversized aquarium, and the very Western, full-sized bar. The bird aviaries were at either end of the front veranda and positioned on the northeast and southeast corners of the house. Since the caged birds could see the outside world, I felt it must be so sad for them to watch the wild birds fly free. I would always remember those aviaries as being my first lesson in the meaning of captivity; my need for freedom resonated painfully with what I considered to be their torture.

Both of my parents loved animals, so we always had a menagerie of pets. Our exotic pets included an ocelot, a monkey, a raccoon, a Mina bird, parrots, a deer, a rabbit, a duck, and even a chicken. Daddy won the baby chick and duck for me at the State Fair, and he always said those were the most expensive fowls on earth. My uncle Jackie dabbled in the animal import business so it was not uncommon to have lions, bears, or panthers to play with on a regular basis. Daddy had his eight hunting dogs that lived in the kennels as well as his Jones Terriers that lived at the house. They were serious skunk chasers and smelled terrible most of the time, so Daddy built them kennels that opened up both to the inside and outside of the house, with removable doors that could be opened or shut to keep them in or out. My mother had her toy poodles, of course, and they were the only animals to have free run of the house. Daddy said if they ever tangled with the ocelot, my mother might rethink her decision. But then Sissy, the oldest poodle, won his heart, so he didn't say too much more about their constant yapping. Daddy gave me a precious Britney Spaniel that ended up being a chicken killer and ate almost all of the ranch foreman's chickens. He went to dog school twice to break him of the habit, but Daddy said, "Once a chicken killer, always a chicken killer," and unfortunately, he was right.

I loved all of our pets, but the exotic animals taught me that wild things are not meant to be in captivity; they are meant to be free in the environment where they were born. When I learned that truth I refused to go to zoos anymore. I saw them as nothing but glorified prisons displaying sad, deranged creatures that had been locked up too long.

The aquarium, located upstairs in the playroom, was six feet long with a rounded leather lounge built in front of it. I called it the "poof" and would lay on it for hours, daydreaming and watching the angelfish, the bottom feeders, the ceramic mermaids, and especially the diver with bubbles coming out of his helmet as he stood over his sunken treasure.

Our house was a National Geographic treasure for a child with an active imagination and an affinity for other cultures. Almost every room in the house had a distinctive decorative theme, and I could drift from room to room, allowing my mood to guide me. The guest rooms included the Mexican room, the Western room, the Hunt room, and Electra's room, which housed most of my grandmother's most prized possessions. The front veranda showcased the bird aviaries with lush tropical plants and Lalique paintings on velvet, completing the Polynesian motif.

The living room was very much a game room, prominently displaying Daddy's gun collection and a huge moose over the fireplace. The upstairs playroom was very eclectic but the predominant themes were African and Native American, highlighted by a twenty-five-foot Navajo rug in red, black, gray, and white. The dining room was pure Ranch style with two dining room tables—one for entertaining guests, and the other, a smaller round table, for just the family. Both had glass tops resting on leather and calf skin bases, with matching chairs. Beautifully hand-painted plates depicting the antics of a frisky young colt and other more sedate equine legends lined the walls. An enormous picture window looked out over a large expanse of old oak trees, lush grass and flowers, deer sculptures, a large bird bath, and countless bird feeders hanging from the trees. Daddy and I loved our quiet mornings there, watching the birds, rabbits, and squirrels while the dew was still on the grass and the house was quiet.

With such an extraordinary world to explore, it was only natural for me to orchestrate my own safaris, creating a variety of exciting foreign adventures. Oddly enough, it was only after I had easy access to other children that I came to realize that I was really a solitary soul, often choosing to be alone. I loved people but I only seemed to be able to enjoy them in small doses and would then retreat to my own fantasy world in order to renew myself. I have never known if that was just my nature to seek solitude or if my life honed that tendency in me out of necessity. Either way, it was a skill that would serve me well throughout my life, and I was comfortable with the sweet melancholy that comes with being alone.

Aerial photo of the ranch house

Ranch house from the back lawn

Moose head in living room

Decorated bear in Rita's playroom

Bar in pool cabana with saddle stools

CHAPTER 19

Camp Waldemar

Age Six

At the end of the school year I started camp at Waldemar, the premier camp for girls in Hunt, Texas, near Kerrville. It was a beautiful place situated on the Guadalupe River, shaded by giant cypress and oak trees. Most of the buildings were made of river rock and were nestled among the trees going up the hill. All of the buildings were connected by stone paths that ran throughout the camp.

My first cabin was called The Dollhouse. It overlooked the amphitheater where we watched a movie every Friday night and got to have a candy bar as a special treat. Normally, we were not allowed to have candy, soft drinks, gum, or even chew ice because it was bad for our teeth and unladylike. Everything about the camp was first class and well thought-out. Connie Reeves, a famous cowgirl who was later inducted into the Cowgirl Hall of Fame, ran the camp and taught all of the riding classes. She was the only real cowgirl I had ever seen up close, and I was awestruck by her beauty and her riding skills. She was lean and brown from the sun with a snowy white head of hair cropped short that framed her pretty face like a halo. Her piercing blue eyes could twinkle with mischief or shoot daggers at you. She wasn't much of a talker, but her presence was something to be reckoned with. Because of my riding skills, I became one of her protégées and felt very privileged to have her as a mentor. I knew she had to be pretty old, but she was still doing trick-riding and I was impressed.

Unfortunately, my parents were not as impressed with trick-riding as I was. It was called "monkey drill" at Waldemar and involved doing acrobatics on a horse while in a full gallop. It was exciting and dangerous, and I was honored to make the team at such a young age. When I boasted to my mother that I would be at the top of the human pyramid due to my size and weight, I thought she was going to have a seizure. For once, she put her foot down and demanded that I withdraw from the team immediately. I was even more shocked when Daddy backed her up by saying, "Squirrel, after weighing the risks, I can't see that it's worth it. What would you use it for?" I couldn't think of a single thing, and knowing Daddy's love of purpose and function, I gave up and started scouting out some of the other activities.

Waldemar offered classes in archery, rifle shooting, swimming, diving, canoeing, pottery, photography, art, trick roping, tennis, and golf. Over the six summers I spent there, I tried almost all of them, but my favorites were canoeing, photography, and tennis. My family was extremely relieved when I stopped taking pottery because they had all been inundated with crudely made bowls, ashtrays, busts, and even alligators that I had made and put in the kiln myself. Ever faithful, Mama and Avis used them around the house for years. That is true love.

There was only one mandatory class at Waldemar. It was called Posture, and we occasionally put books on our heads in order to learn to walk properly, but for all practical purposes, it was one of the first exercise/stretch classes designed specifically for women. Our teacher's name was Roe and she was the oldest-looking human I had ever seen. She looked like a witch out of a fairy tale and I was a little afraid when I first saw her. Her body was almost bent in half and her hands were gnarly claws, twisted from crippling arthritis.

While we worked out under the pavilion in the middle of the quadrangle, she sat in a chair and lectured us in her strong, raspy voice, "Ladies, do you want to look like me? I don't think so. Well, then, keep exercising. Don't ever quit, no matter what good excuses you come up with. And, ladies, it's okay to work up a sweat. You'll be glad you did when you're my age."

Roe was ahead of her time and dared to promote exercise for women long before it was fashionable. I have always been grateful and proud to be one of "Roe's girls," and I took her words to heart, exercising almost every day of my life.

Waldemar also sought to instill old-fashioned moral fiber and integrity in its girls and, for better or worse, used Native American traditions to try to achieve this. When a girl entered camp, she became either an Aztec, a Comanche, or a Téjas. Each tribe had its own color, chief, and tribal hill.

There was fierce rivalry between the tribes, and at the end of the competitions, the tribe with the most awards won the grand prize. But for me, the most inspirational and ethereal moments began with our silent, solemn journey up to our tribal hill. Once there, we softly sang our tribal song and asked for the Great Spirit to make us better and stronger, as we gazed in wonder at the brilliant stars hanging in the night sky and watched the sparks from the fire dance around us.

The only thing that could rival the hilltop inspiration was the Ideal Girl ceremony. Every session, a girl was chosen for that award because she personified all of the highest ideals that Waldemar represented. It was held by firelight beside the river, and the "ideal girl" was dressed in a white shirt and shorts with a solid-white feather headdress that touched the ground. At first, she was shrouded in darkness on the platform overlooking the river, but as her name was called out and we sang the "ideal girl" song, a spotlight fell on her and the fires were lit. Even my mother teared up during that ceremony, which was saying a lot because all she could really think about right then was her discomfort from our trek up the hill. Having never gone to camp ceremonies before, she arrived in full polo regalia—white linen sheath and spiked heels.

Watching her gamely struggle up that rocky hill in the dark, wearing high heels, endeared her to me. And as an added bonus, I had climbed up the totem pole of popularity because all of the girls thought my mother looked like a movie star, which she did, of course.

CHAPTER 20

Kitchen Gossip

Age Six

The first place I went when I got home was the kitchen. I always loved it there because of the happy chatter and the good smells, but it was also the place to go if you wanted to know all of the latest gossip. I couldn't wait to find out if Little Bill, our handsome young waiter, had gotten into any more fights over Mel, one of the pretty waitresses. Miss Mandy and Rosie said she might be the color of honey but she was slower than molasses, and then they would cackle like crazy enjoying their little joke. Mel had trained under all of the older women, but none of them felt she was suited to anything except waiting tables and there was always a lively discussion about how she could improve herself.

I asked Miss Mandy if she thought all that kidding ever hurt Mel's feelings. She laughed and said, "Lord, no, chil'. Most of what we say goes right over her head. It's a good thing she's pretty, 'cause she dumber than a fence post."

As I stood looking at Mel now, I thought she was more ethereal than dumb, but Dorothy was just giving her a lecture on finding herself a *real* Black man, not some milk-coffee-colored weakling like herself.

Miss Mandy was mixed-race, as well, but no one ever dared say anything like that to her. Rosie snorted and said, "She done missed her chance with that good-looking mechanic that works at the shop. Now he be African Black, and Lordy, chil', what a pretty man."

Anxious to be helpful, I said, "Maybe it's not too late." Rosie looked sad and then said, "Oh, you weren't here. He done gone and caught himself on fire. He nearly burnt to death before they could catch him and throw him to the ground. Poor thing, it was just awful. They said he had gasoline on his clothes and a spark from his cigarette set him on fire. He ain't pretty no more."

Something squeezed tight in my heart when I heard the story because I knew what it was like to be burned, and it was hard enough without people telling you that you weren't pretty anymore. I remembered seeing him working on the trucks down at the shop, but he was a quiet man and I didn't know him very well. I had lost interest in the conversation and felt strangely compelled to go see him. He was bending over an engine when I approached and did not see me until I tugged on his trousers. Looking at me in surprise, he squatted down to my eye level. He saw me studying the large pink and white splotches erupting from his skin and self-consciously looked away.

I reached out a tentative finger to touch his face gently, and asked, "Does it hurt?"

He smiled sadly, and said, "Not anymore."

Looking him square in the eyes, I said, "I got burned, too. Did you know that?"

A solemn look came over his face. "I heard about that," he said. "I'm sorry."

"It's okay," I said, pulling my shirt back so he could see the scars on my shoulder and neck.

He gently reached out and touched my shoulder, asking, "Does it hurt?"

"Not anymore," I answered. "I just wanted to tell you what my grandmother told me. Pretty is as pretty does. You're still the same person and Jesus will always love you."

He took my hands in his and said, "I sure enough do appreciate you sharing that with me and I won't ever forget it."

As I walked away, I turned back to him and said, "Oh, and I still think you're pretty . . . kinda like a zebra, black-and-white."

Upon returning to the house, I stopped short when I heard my parents talking about me. My mother was saying she was very concerned about how much time I spent with the servants and the cowboys. "Buster, just listening to her, you would swear she was Black, and God only knows what language she's picked up from the cowboys."

Daddy chuckled, and said, "She's a great mimic. She only sounds like that when she wants to. And as far as the cowboys go, they adore her and would never do or say anything inappropriate around her. I think you're worrying over nothing, but what do you suggest we do?"

"Well, Electra says their governess, Pat, has a friend in England who might be interested in coming here. Supposedly, her credentials are impeccable and I think Rita could stand a little polish. If you agree, I thought I would give her a call."

Daddy shrugged, and said, "That sounds fine to me. Do whatever you think is best but make sure she understands, Rita is not your typical child. I don't want her leaving here like a scalded cat as soon as she gets a load of our little squirrel."

Mother grimaced and said, "Oh, I'm sure Pat will give her an earful about the whole family. I don't think we have to worry about her arriving with any illusions."

After hearing that conversation, I knew my days of freedom were numbered, and even though I wasn't sure what "governess" meant, it sounded pretty highfalutin to me.

CHAPTER 21

Bucky's Visit

Age Six

That evening at dinner, when Daddy told me my stepbrother, Bucky, was coming for a short visit, I was ecstatic. He was absolutely adorable, with sandy blonde hair and languid, green cat-eyes that sported the longest lashes I had ever seen. He was two years younger than me and I loved having a little brother, even though we were very different. He didn't like horses or guns and preferred to be inside playing with his erector set. I figured it was because he didn't come to the ranch often enough to get used to those things.

Mother was not the least disappointed, because now she had someone to keep her company when Daddy and I were out. Oddly enough, Mother seemed to feel a stronger kinship with Bucky than with me, and the four of us fell into a comfortable pattern of companionship. I spent most of my time outside with Daddy, and Bucky spent most of his time inside with Mother.

This trip was going to be different though, because Daddy said he intended to teach Bucky to swim. Mother didn't say anything, but I could tell by her slight frown that she was as concerned as I was. Bucky had screamed bloody murder when Daddy put him on a horse and showed him my shotgun. The few times he had been around the pool, he had clung to Mother and shown no interest in getting in the water. Mother was also afraid of the water and horses, so she had great sympathy and was very protective of Bucky. I just hoped Daddy wouldn't try to teach him like he taught me, but that is what eventually happened.

First, Daddy tried walking around the shallow end, holding Bucky in his arms, but you would have thought the water was liquid fire the way Bucky screamed and tried to keep his feet from touching the water. Thoroughly frustrated, Daddy resorted to what he knew best. Prying Bucky's little hands from around his neck, he threw him into the deep end and said, "Swim!"

I will never forget the look of sheer terror on Bucky's face as he hit the water and quickly sank to the bottom. A few horrifying seconds passed before Daddy said, "Go get your brother." I dove into the water, grabbed Bucky, and burst to the surface where Daddy pulled him out. The minute his feet hit the tile, he was running toward the house, screaming like a banshee.

I had never seen Daddy look so defeated, but he shook his head and said, "Deets, go see if you can find out what's wrong with him." I passed Mother on the way to the house, and by the look on her face, there was going to be hell to pay.

I found Bucky curled up in the fetal position behind the bed and began crooning to him and stroking him the way Mama did with me when I was upset. He finally grew quiet and I asked him why he was so afraid of the water. In between sniffles, he told me why he was terrified of horses, guns, and water, and I was so shocked I didn't know what to say. After he fell into an exhausted sleep, I went to tell Daddy what I had found out.

Daddy looked a little singed from the tongue-lashing Mother had given him but was eager to hear my report. Crawling onto his lap, I said, "He's afraid because his mother told him horses, guns, and water would kill him." The look on Daddy's face was as if someone had punched him in the stomach. He took a deep breath and hung his head. Now, even more confused, I asked, "Why would she do that, Daddy?"

He let out a long sigh, and said, "Why, indeed?" I waited as he digested this new information and finally, he said, "Thanks for helping your brother today. Now that we know what's wrong, we'll just have to be very patient with him. You'll be a big help in showing him those things won't hurt him. You'll do that for him, won't you, honey?"

"Sure, Daddy," I replied. "I just don't ever want to see him that scared again." "Me too," he said as we walked back to the house.

Sure enough, with a little time and patience, he was riding, shooting, and swimming with the best of them, but I would never forget what that poor little boy went through, and what courage it took to overcome his fears.

CHAPTER 22

Circus

Age Seven

Later that year, Mother and Daddy took me to see the Ringling Brothers Circus in Fort Worth. Knowing how I loved animals and make-believe, they just knew it would be one of the highlights of my short life. At first, I loved it. I was entranced by the lights, music, animals, and colorful people. With three rings to choose from, I hardly knew which act to watch first. I could tell the animals were smart and well trained because they weren't afraid of fire. The lions and tigers leaped through flaming rings and I was very impressed. The elephants looked so happy with their big ears flapping jauntily as they raced around the outer circle. Beautiful girls in sparkling costumes rode on their backs, and I longed to be one of those girls. Pretty ladies and handsome men in their glittering, tight costumes flew through the air on their trapeze swings high above, and I squealed when they let themselves drop to the safety net at the end of their performance.

Had we left immediately after the show, I would have said I liked circuses, but Daddy knew one of the clowns so he took me backstage to meet him. He thought he was doing something special for me, but that was where my disillusionment began. As we walked through the curtained doorway, a horrible smell assaulted my nostrils and my eyes watered from the rank stench of urine, sweat, and sawdust. Next, I saw the dancing elephants I had so admired in chains around one ankle, their heads hung low in misery. There were bloody wounds around their ankles where they had pulled and pulled against the metal trying to free themselves. Then came the fearless lions and tigers, but they were no longer majestic or brave. They paced their cages with frenzied repetition and their eyes had the haunted, vacant look of all captive wild things. I was near tears and pulling back on Daddy's hand as we made our way to his friend's tent. Looking back at me reassuringly, he led me past the animals and into the performers' area.

I could not believe that these were the same people I had just watched in the show. The women looked coarse and tired, their faces caked in make-up and their costumes shabby when seen up close. I was reeling by the time Daddy pulled me into his friend's tent, but I was determined to be polite despite his scary appearance. He had removed half of his makeup and I could smell the pungent rags that littered the dresser in front of him. Daddy coaxed me to give him a hug but I stood rooted to the ground, eyes wide and breathing hard. His kind eyes registered understanding, and he said, "It's okay, Bus. I'm a stranger. We'll get to know each other when I come for a visit."

I was so relieved I could have kissed him but instead, I hung my head and acted shy for one of the few times in my life. Finally, we left and just as Daddy was asking what was wrong with me, I began to throw up all of the cotton candy, peanuts, and cokes that I had consumed in the last few hours. He assumed my odd behavior was due to a stomachache and I never told him the truth. Nevertheless, from that day forward, I refused to go to another circus and that behind-the-scenes experience later generalized to other areas of my life, making me regret looking too closely behind any too-good-to-be-true facades.

CHAPTER 23

The Kind Mistress

Age Eight

When I was eight, my paternal grandmother, Rena, came from California and Charles arranged for me to spend a few days with him in Dallas. I didn't know her very well, and he wanted to remedy that before I got any older. She took care of me when he had business to attend to, but things weren't going too well. Looking over my shoulder as I practiced writing my name, she reacted vehemently to what I had written. In a very displeased voice she said, "That is not your name. Write your real name."

Confused, but wanting to please her, I dutifully did as she said, and wrote, "Rita Link." When Daddy got home and asked where I was, she replied, "She's in her room. Probably telling Jesus what a bad grandmother I am." Daddy chuckled and kissed her on the cheek, asking, "What happened?"

She recounted the name incident and Daddy, frowning thoughtfully, said, "Mother, Rita doesn't understand the legality of all that and I would appreciate it if you wouldn't make a big deal out of it. Buster and I will work all of that out when she's older."

Lifting her chin defiantly, Rena said, "It's not just that, Charles. She's a very strange child. What do you do with her? She doesn't like zoos or the circus, and her best friend is Jesus. Who ever heard of such?"

Using his most conciliatory tone, he replied, "Well, she doesn't like to see animals caged, and a lot of children have imaginary friends, Mother."

Scandalized, she said, "But Jesus, for crying out loud. I think it's all very weird. What will people think?"

Trying to control his irritation, Daddy laughed and said, "It could be worse. She could have chosen Satan."

Aghast, she snapped back, "This is no laughing matter, Charles. What on earth is Buster teaching that child?"

Suddenly serious, Daddy gripped her shoulders gently and looked at her intently, saying, "Buster is doing a fine job, and Rita is not weird or strange. She is exceptional, and I hope you will allow yourself to see that before you leave."

Daddy seldom challenged her, but she heard the note of finality in his voice and wisely chose to retreat. Overhearing that conversation, I learned a very valuable lesson. I wasn't sure why, but most people were not comfortable when I talked about Jesus so I began to keep our relationship a secret, except from a few trusted people.

Daddy walked into my room, leaned down to kiss me, and said, "Hello, my darling girl. What would you like to do this afternoon?" He was the only person I knew that used the word "darling" and I loved the sound of it, the way it looked in his letters to me which always began, "My Darling," in his large, sprawling script. Leaping into his arms, I thought for a minute, and then my face lit up as I asked, "Can we visit the nice lady who lives at the lake?" He threw back his head in laughter, then threw me into the air and said, "You never cease to amaze me, you little minx. I'll call her and see if it's convenient."

On the way to Fort Worth, Daddy seemed deep in thought but he finally winked at me and said, "Darling, I think it would be best if we kept these visits our little secret. Could we do that?" I was beginning to realize that there were a lot of secrets in the grown-up world, so I said, "Sure, Daddy. I can keep a secret."

Upon our arrival, she greeted us in her usual, warm manner and directed Daddy to where her "husband" sat by the lake. No one was allowed to smoke in her house, and it always smelled like fresh-cut flowers. She looked elegant and beautiful, as always, even though she was really old, a lot older than Daddy, I was sure. Smiling at me, she crooked her finger and I followed her into the kitchen, anticipating our little ritual.

She always served high tea or mint juleps in the afternoon, depending on the season. As I watched her prepare the tray, I felt like I was watching an artist at work and I greatly admired her culinary skills and her genteel manner. Once comfortably settled on the love seat, delicately sipping our tea, her blue eyes twinkling like a young girl's, she smiled at me and said, "Tell me everything."

She listened attentively as I told her all the news I had, occasionally laughing or nodding sympathetically. When it was time to go she kissed me and said, "Please come see me again soon. I so love your visits."

Somehow knowing I could trust her, I leaned toward her and whispered, "So do I. And Jesus really likes it here, too." She put her hand to her mouth as her eyes filled with tears and in a husky voice she said, "I'm very glad to hear that."

It would be years before I really understood who that beautiful lady was and why my words had made her cry. She was the life-long mistress of a friend of Daddy's, and that lovely little house by the lake was their peaceful refuge from a cruel world and a vengeful wife who would not give him a divorce. Even though they were old, they were still very much in love and their love made them young. I wondered if anyone would ever look at me the way he looked at her. I was fourteen the last time I saw her and she seemed to know that it would be our last visit. Holding my face in her hands, memorizing every detail, she said, "You have been the daughter I could never have. Thank you for that. Stay sweet and be happy." When we got to the door, she handed me a beautifully wrapped gift, and said, "To remember me by."

Once in the car, I opened it and found a book, entitled, *Advice from an Old Mistress to a Young Bride.* As I held the book to my heart, crying softly, Daddy didn't say a word but reached across and gently held my hand as we drove back to Dallas.

CHAPTER 24

A Good Christmas

Age Eight

Christmas at our house was really something special and no one looked forward to it more than Daddy. He planned his gifts months ahead and always gave himself at least one present that he marked, "From Me, to Me." Mother started planning months ahead, too, because the tree and all the decorations had to be ordered months in advance. The tree was always at least ten feet tall, reaching to the ceiling of the living room. The moose, the bear, and all of the other trophies had to have wreaths around their necks and sparkly masks. Live greenery was draped along the banister, and there were Christmas centerpieces on every table.

Winking at me, Daddy would say, "Deets, don't stand around in here too long or you'll get decorated." He was a big kid when it came to Christmas, and he made it fun for everyone. He bought Mother a pair of earrings one year, but he put them inside bigger and bigger boxes until the box was the size of a large television. Every time Mother passed the box, she would frown and say, "I can't believe he got me a TV." Daddy got weeks of chuckles out of that little prank. He loved riddles, too, so at least one of his presents to me could only be located by following a series of riddles leading me around the house on a treasure hunt. Mother and Daddy put Bucky's presents on the south end of the veranda and mine on the north end, just to make sure there would be no squabbles over what belonged to whom. I must admit, when we were very young, I was jealous of the fancy, red fire truck that could really pump water and the bright, yellow crane that could lift buckets of dirt, but I eventually reconciled myself to more feminine gifts.

Every year Mother and Daddy had a party at our house on Christmas Eve while Bucky and I celebrated with all the aunts, uncles, and cousins at my grandmother's house in town. The Irish are a rowdy bunch, always looking for an excuse to have a good time, and I could never picture my more sedate, English grandfather tolerating the mayhem that took place every year. There were always fireworks and, inevitably, the older kids and my uncles would end up in a firecracker fight. Mama was never happier than when she was surrounded by her large brood and she beamed proudly as she presided over her clan. She pretended not to see the dog eating off the table and smiled tolerantly when her grandchildren climbed on her, wiping their sticky fingers on her good dress. She only intervened once that I could remember and that was the year my uncles gave all the kids cigars to smoke. Ten children retching at the same time was more than she could bear, and our only consolation was in watching her chastise our tormentors.

"What's wrong with you? Have you lost your minds? Look at these poor children. So, what do you have to say for yourselves?" Sick as we were, we gleefully watched as she reduced grown men into sniveling boys, stumbling over their own feet as they mumbled, "Sorry, Ma."

We were usually out like a light by the time Mother and Daddy arrived to take us home and rarely woke up until Daddy started ringing the cow bell at the crack of dawn. It usually took him about thirty minutes to round us all up, shouting "Merry Christmas," as we each sat staring at him, bleary-eyed. Mother wasn't at her best before she'd had her coffee, and I admired her restraint as she tried to muster some Christmas cheer. Just the family, which included Grace or Joyce, my eventual English governess, opened our presents first. As soon as we were finished, Daddy went to work on his infamous Christmas Toddy. He filled a large punch bowl with eggnog, poured in a fifth of whiskey, added a gallon of vanilla ice cream, and then liberally sprinkled nutmeg on the surface. Some of the top hands would arrive soon afterward to open their presents and knowing the eggnog would be their first stop, he did not want to disappoint them. By the time the presents had been distributed and the eggnog was gone, those boys were ready to play.

Under the pretense of showing us how to ride our new bikes or whatever the new toys might be, they would stumble around, falling all over each other, laughing their fool heads off, with an occasional, "Excuse me, Ma'am," whenever my mother made an appearance. Daddy's defense was always the same, "They work hard all year. They deserve a little fun at Christmas," but he shouldn't have bothered because we all got a kick out of watching those grown men playing like a bunch of schoolboys.

Rita and Bucky at Christmastime

Bucky on toy cruiser

White Christmas tree at ranch

CHAPTER 25

The Gypsies Arrive

Age Nine

The year I turned nine was a banner year in many ways, but the event that most captivated me was the arrival of the gypsies. Daddy got word that they were camped down at Beaver Creek and when he headed that way, we all assumed that he would run them off like most of the other ranchers. Everyone said *they're nothing but a pack of thieves*, but something about them touched a chord in Daddy and he decided to give them a chance. He laid out his terms with their leader and they shook hands on it: no stealing, no killing of the white-tailed deer, caution with their fires, and Daddy would give them one or two cows, depending on their need. Everyone thought Daddy had lost his mind and assured him that they would rob him blind. Daddy didn't really care what anyone else thought, but he defended his decision by saying, "A man with a full belly is less likely to steal."

However, just in case he was wrong, he personally moved them to a more private site near Hoot 'N Hollar Bridge, where they would have good water and more room to spread out. When I asked Daddy why he had let them stay, he was quiet for a minute and then, looking sad, he said, "They're kinda like cowboys and Indians. Free spirits hankering to roam, but there's not much open space left for them anymore. Most of the land's been bought up and covered with barbed wire. It's too late for the Indians and it won't be long before the cowboys are gone, too, but I can at least give these people a place to light for a while."

Daddy never regretted that kindness and he spent many an enjoyable evening at their campfire. He and their leader developed a real respect for one another and I knew Daddy really trusted them when he showed them where to hunt the wild pigs.

Of course, I was dying to get to see them and constantly badgered Daddy with questions. Mother had forbidden me to go near them, but Daddy finally convinced her that I would lose interest once I had seen them. That was not the case, but his line of reasoning got me into their camp and that was all I cared about. I was a little disappointed to see so many cars instead of horses and gypsy wagons, but Daddy said modern times were catching up with everyone.

I soon forgot my disappointment when the music began and I met some of the children. They had the best fiddler I had ever heard and everyone, including the children, danced to that haunting music with wild abandon. I was enthralled with their beauty amid the vivid colors, but most of all I admired their zest for life.

I could tell they took huge bites out of life; there was no dainty nibbling for these people. Even though I was not allowed to visit them again, I never forgot them and sometimes I thought I could hear their music drifting on the wind as I lay quiet in my bed. Daddy understood my fascination, and when he gave me my first stereo and several of his favorite albums, one of them was entitled *Gypsy Caravans.* I loved that record because it conjured up all of the exotic sights and sounds of my one magical night with the gypsies, enabling me to relive those intoxicating hours again and again.

CHAPTER 26

A Room of My Own

Age Nine

The biggest milestone of the year was getting my very own room. I was a big girl now, at least age-wise, and Mother hired an architect to add a new bedroom, dressing room, and bathroom just for me. Thinking ahead to the formidable teenage years, Daddy suggested he build a new playroom for me and Bucky as well. My room was all pale pink with white eyelet organdy drapes that covered the two walls of windows. There was a large canopy bed, a French Provincial grandmother's clock my parents had picked up in Hot Springs, Arkansas, a long dresser with numerous drawers, a lovely two-foot tall geisha girl encased in glass, and several comfortable chairs. My toy stuffed animals filled up all the space in between and stood guard like castle sentinels when I slept alone for the first time. It was not as scary I had thought it might be, and I actually found that it gave me that new sense of freedom that comes with maturity.

Our new playroom was large and comfortable, with a working fireplace, a long expanse of built-in cabinets and drawers, two large benches that converted into a ping-pong table, bookshelves for my ever-growing book collection, a mirrored cabinet for my doll collection, a piano, a television, and a stereo. My friends thought it odd that I would have a doll collection, but each doll represented a country my parents had visited. Their unique features and costumes were an endless source of delight to me, whetting my imagination and transporting me to their world. My favorite was an Eskimo girl dressed in a fur snowsuit that made me dream of whales, polar bears, and igloos. Every time my parents went on a trip, I eagerly awaited my new foreign friend who would come to share their world with me.

My new living quarters fulfilled every fantasy a girl could wish for, but I was even more intrigued by the bonus feature I had not anticipated: the freedom to come and go as I pleased, even at night. My wing of the house was at the opposite end of my parents' and I had my own private entrance. The possibilities were endless, and I explored every one of them before I left home for good.

CHAPTER 27

Lady Godiva

Age Nine

My first excursions into freedom were moonlit walks down to my secret place at the pond. From my bench there I could see the great rugged landscape bathed in moonlight, which at night looked softer somehow, almost surreal. Everything seemed to shimmer in a soft blue haze. If I focused really hard, I could see coyotes running in the distance and sense the rabbits as they nibbled on the greenery around me. The night was filled with a symphony of insects and I listened closely to identify individual songs. I knew each of them intimately and it was comforting to be serenaded by such familiar sounds. Human energy could be so discordant and draining, but I always found the music of nature peaceful.

Gazing at the moon, I wondered if you could feel moonlight on your skin, and that thought led me to discover a new passion: being naked in nature, especially at night. Taking off my nightie, I lay stretched out on the soft grass, watching the heavens sparkle above me, and I knew I was one with all of nature. Sometimes, overcome by the sheer beauty and grandeur, I could taste the salty liquid in my mouth as I smiled through my tears.

I loved the newfound freedom of my night walks, but it was not long before I got an even better idea. Daddy had given me a set of books containing true and sometimes spectacular stories from history. They often included images of the people involved, and I was captivated by the painting of Lady Godiva. She was a woman, a little chubby I thought, with very long hair, who decided to go horseback riding naked. Her hair covered most of her body so you couldn't see anything important, but I just could not figure out why she wanted to ride through the middle of town like that.

The idea of riding naked had never occurred to me, but I thought it was a grand idea if I made a couple of alterations: I would ride naked, shielded by the cover of night.

Thus began my night rides instead of walks, and my need for freedom escalated once again. My first attempt was a little harrowing because I was afraid the hunting dogs or peacocks would give me away when I got Cinco out of his stall. The peacocks huffed and rustled their feathers but they never screamed. I crept to the kennels and spoke softly to each of the dogs, promising to bring them a treat on my next excursion. All of the critters quickly adapted to my night rides and I grew more confident as time passed. One night, however, I got a real wake-up call when I heard someone coming up from behind me. Listening intently, I could tell they were on horseback and riding at a leisurely pace. I could not imagine who would be out there in the middle of the night, so I reined my horse in among the branches of a tree and stood dead still waiting to see who would come around the bend. I stroked Cinco's neck to calm him but I was terrified as I watched the rider come into view. I knew he was a good tracker because he had slowed his pace, which meant he knew I had stopped.

My heart beat wildly as I held my breath, waiting to see who followed me. Suddenly, he came out of the shadows and I breathed a sigh of relief; I would know that shape anywhere, it was just Daddy. He was scanning the darkness for me when I rode out from the shelter of the tree. His eyes widened slightly when he saw me but he just said, "Hey, Deets. What-cha doing?"

"Riding," I answered blithely. "Isn't it a great night for a ride, Daddy?"

At a loss for words, he mumbled, "Umm-hum. Yes, it is. But why are you naked?"

Giving him a big smile, I said, "Don't you know? I'm Lady Godiva."

Daddy digested that information for a moment, then finally said, "Didn't she ride through a town? It's a lot more dangerous out here. What if your horse spooked or stepped in a hole?"

Looking somewhat contrite, I said, "I didn't think about that. I just thought it was a great idea, but that she must have been a hussy for doing it in broad daylight in the middle of town. Was I wrong, Daddy?"

Trying to cover his smile, he said, "No. No, you weren't wrong. She probably was a hussy and I sure don't want you doing anything like that. But my main concern is safety. What if Cinco was spooked by a rattler and accidently threw you off and you had to get home on foot, naked, in the daylight? That would be pretty embarrassing, wouldn't it?"

My eyes grew as big as saucers as I pictured that happening, and I whispered, "Yes, it would. I would never live it down with the cowboys."

Daddy chuckled and said, "Well, if it was me, I'd be a lot more concerned about what your mother might have to say, but that's just me. I'll tell you what. Whenever you get a hankering for a night ride I'll go with you, but I won't ride naked."

Giggling, I said, "Oh, Daddy. You'd look so funny."

He tried to sound offended. "You look pretty funny yourself. At least your hair's grown long enough to cover most of your body. You know, I don't think I've ever seen anyone naked on a horse before."

We headed back to the barn. Daddy finally broke the silence and said, "Isn't riding naked kinda uncomfortable?"

"Well, I tried bareback first, but that was really uncomfortable. It's not bad now that I found that cotton blanket."

Shaking his head, he said, "It just doesn't seem practical to me."

CHAPTER 28

The Governess

Age Nine

Even though Daddy never reprimanded me about my night rides, I could tell that even he thought Joyce was arriving not a moment too soon. I had mixed emotions, but I was curious to see what an English governess looked like. I was shocked when I saw her because she was nothing like I had pictured. She was almost six feet tall with flaming red hair and covered with freckles. I was wondering how her fair skin would handle the Texas sun, when she came striding toward me with an outstretched hand. "Hello, Rita. I'm Joyce. I hope we will be good friends."

Regaining my composure, I shook her hand and said, "It's nice to meet you." Introductions dispensed with, she said, "Why don't you show me around and we can get acquainted."

She did not seem too old, early thirties maybe, but she sure enough was a take-charge kind of person. I studied her as we walked and I knew there would be no crying or moping around for this woman. As I got to know her better, I realized that was an understatement; she would have chewed her arm off before she would have let anyone see her cry. Her merry blue eyes took in everything, and it was obvious that not much daunted this woman. She was not beautiful in the traditional way but her personality and presence made her very attractive. I began to notice that she also walked in a very jaunty manner, with a little hop. It would be months before I knew why. She had been born with a slightly deformed foot, but she did not let a little thing like that stop her. She was very British, with a stiff upper lip, and did not think anyone should feel sorry for themselves, least of all herself.

Her swimming skills would have put Esther Williams to shame, and she was a wicked adversary on the tennis court. I was the lucky recipient of those skills even though I could never duplicate her masterful ease in the water. Her powerful strokes hardly made a ripple and her breathing was perfect. Little did I know that one day my life would depend on her extraordinary skills and the strenuous training she put me though. In order to build strength in my legs, she made me kick at the side of the pool for hours, and when I swam laps, I could hear her yelling, "Reach, Rita. Reach. Breathe. Don't fake it."

Joyce was a natural athlete and one of the most upbeat, can-do people I had ever met. She approached everything with the same gusto, including my discipline. Patience was not her strong suit, and if I refused to eat everything on my plate she would rap my knuckles with her knife and tell me horrific stories of the food shortage in London due to the relentless German bombings. Those stories of hungry children imprinted themselves on my soul and I suffered massive guilt whenever I left food on my plate. She also told me she had worked with "the underground" during the war and for years, I mistakenly pictured her jauntily hopping through miles of underground tunnels.

All in all, my parents were absolutely thrilled with Joyce and felt sure she would take me in hand and make a lady out of me yet. And to her credit, she did the best job anyone could have done, especially when it came to discipline and duty. Letter writing was an art form to her, and she demanded that I maintain proper correspondence when I was at camp and later, when I was away at school. She also insisted that I send out timely thank-you notes and my own Christmas cards to school friends. Being thrifty, she taught me to collect coupon stamps and introduced me to the joy of giving my family and friends gifts obtained by redeeming those stamps.

My all-time favorite was the electric blanket I got for Miss Mandy. She said it made her old bones feel so much better, and you would have thought I had given her a million dollars by the look on her face.

Joyce was a high-spirited, friendly person so she fit right in at the ranch, despite being so British. She was game for almost anything and eager to learn everything there was to know about ranch life. When my parents were out of town, we went to all of the fish fries, barbecues, and dined regularly at the chuck wagon. Cookie, the camp cook, made the best sourdough rolls and peach cobbler you ever ate, and the coffee was just right, so strong you could stand a spoon up in it.

At some point, I began to suspect that Joyce was interested in more than just the good eats and friendly socializing. She had her eye on Eddie Browder but he was plainly scared to death of her. He had never encountered such a forward woman and turned scarlet and got tongue-tied whenever she came near him. I was not sure how they were going to get to know each other, but I needn't have worried. Joyce had a plan, and she began a relentless siege on that unsuspecting cowboy.

Almost every day, after she picked me up at school, she would pull up in front of the bunkhouse and sit on the horn. I was horrified the first time she did it because I knew the cowboys had been up since three or four in the morning and often took a nap before dinner. Embarrassed, I slid down in my seat and informed her that this was unseemly and inconsiderate. "Nonsense," she chirped. "They are grown men and have no business lolling around in bed at this time of day."

Eddie would come dragging out of the bunkhouse, bleary-eyed and barefoot, motioning for her to quit honking the horn. Leaning on my door and winking at me, he said, "Hi, Rita, Joyce. What's up?"

Smiling like the cat that ate the canary, she said, "We're inviting you to dinner. You've got fifteen minutes to get ready. Chop. Chop. We'll wait."

Rolling his eyes and looking exhausted, he answered, "Well, gee. Thanks for the invite but I'm not very hungry right now." Joyce looked a bit peeved and said, "You will be. We will not take no for an answer, will we, Rita?"

I looked apologetically at Eddie, shrugged, and scooted down even further in my seat. Weary but resigned, Eddie smiled wanly and said, "I'll be as quick as I can."

Joyce dragged him to movies, dinners, picnics, and God only knows what else and she eventually got her man. Some said she just finally wore him down and others said it was those short shorts she wore on a regular basis. It was a good thing everyone liked Joyce so much because the ranch wives would have been scandalized if anyone else had dared wear anything so revealing. I thought Rosie summed it up quite well when she said, "She sure do love to strut her stuff," and we all said, "Amen."

Joyce Browder, Rita's English governess, and Rita

Eddie Browder, one of the top cowboys on the ranch and Joyce's future husband, and Rita

CHAPTER 29

The Allens Arrive

Age Nine

When Mother and Daddy added the new utility room, a beauty salon was added, as well. This included a salon sink, cabinet and chair, a large mirror, a hair dryer, a manicure table, a steam bath, a massage table, and a sun lamp. This addition was Mother's pride and joy, because now she and her female guests could get their hair done after hunting or a day at the lake. The only thing missing was a hairdresser who would be willing to live at the ranch and be on call as needed.

Daddy was looking for a good tile man to remodel the bathrooms and maintain the tile in the pool. One afternoon, he brought home a man who was highly recommended as a tile layer, and lo and behold, his wife was a hairdresser. They had three children—a girl my age and two boys, one Bucky's age and another slightly younger. They seemed custom-made for the needs of our family, and since Miss Mandy had moved into town after her husband Simp died, they moved into her house right next to ours.

I was especially excited to meet their daughter, Carol, and when we finally met, I could hardly believe my eyes. We could have passed for sisters, except her long hair was slightly more blonde than mine and her skin was a little more olive. We took one look at each other and knew that we had met a kindred spirit. Both of us talking a mile a minute, we jumped on our bikes so I could give her the grand tour. I could hardly believe my good fortune when she told me she loved horses and all of the other things I liked, except for hunting. I had never met another girl like me and we soon became inseparable. We rode horses, biked, swam, fished, careened around in the Green Goose, baked cookies, and told each other our deepest secrets as we hid from the sun under the eaves of the roof on hot summer days.

Joe Props would join us in our more genteel activities like baking or swimming, but he didn't like getting hot and dirty. Joe was gay and the son of our top cowboy, Son Props, and I always had the greatest respect for how he stood up for Joe. He could cook circles around us and we often teased him that he was more girlie-girl than we were. Looking indignant, he would retort, "Well, I should hope so. If it weren't for your long hair, no one would ever guess you were girls."

When Joe was older, he cooked for the chuck wagon at the Four Sixes Ranch, as well as elaborate dinner parties at the "big house" for Little Ann. Occasionally she even flew him to New York City to cook for her big city friends. Joe was the best son any parents could ask for, taking care of them until the day they died. So many cowboys came in from all over the country for Son's funeral that they had to rent the community center. Many of them brought their fiddles, so it was quite a send-off. You haven't lived until you've seen a cowboy's funeral. Joe and I remained close until his untimely death, and I ended up marrying his cousin, Rocky Glasscock.

We didn't care about Joe's jokes regarding our boyishness because we had our feminine moments that he was not privy to. Our favorite game was Jungle Girl. We thought Jane, Tarzan's wife, was just about the luckiest girl in the world. She and Tarzan had their own tree house and a jungle full of animal friends that were always coming to their rescue. We would meet just before dawn and slip naked into the pool where we would pretend we were swimming in a jungle pond beneath a beautiful waterfall. With our long hair spread out all around us, we glided through the water creating new movements for our water ballet. Occasionally, we would sprint to the front of the house to lie down at the top of the hill so we could watch the sunrise. This was a little tricky because we had to time it just right so we wouldn't be caught by the yardmen.

When it was just too hot to be outside, we would sneak one of her dad's "girlie" magazines from under her parents' bed and giggle as we read the lurid stories. Her mother, Dorothy, caught us eventually, and, looking horrified, said, "Those are not fit for any young ladies' eyes. You girls should be ashamed of yourselves."

Dorothy had long red hair, freckles, and was always on a diet, attempting to diminish her short, plump body. I understood why those magazines were a sore point between Kenneth and Dorothy, but I tried to make her feel better by telling her I thought it was just a "guy thing" because my Daddy had them too. She snorted and said she felt sure my Daddy had better taste, and she later confirmed that when I took her one of Daddy's *Playboy* magazines.

Raising an eyebrow as she flipped through the pages, she asked if I was allowed to look at them. I said, "Oh, sure. Daddy keeps them in his bathroom and I look at the pictures while he's shaving. He says real women don't look like that, it's the trick photography, you know, and that I should remember that something left to the imagination has much more mystique and is much more desirable."

Dorothy seemed somewhat mollified, but not quite convinced. "Well, your Daddy is a smart man, but I still don't think you girls should be looking at trashy magazines."

Actually, we weren't all that interested in looking at naked ladies because we much preferred the *True Confession* magazines that Dorothy kept under her side of the bed. We would giggle and blush as we read the juicy parts to each other, speculating on what sex was really all about. We would fantasize about the future and promised each other we would marry friends and live in the apartments over the garage. Every morning, we would cook breakfast in the shared kitchen and raise our babies together.

Life seemed full of glorious possibilities until our brothers would come along and shatter our perfect reveries with their stupid pranks. Because Carol and I were older and better at most things, they took great delight in torturing us with the two things we were both afraid of—bugs and frogs. Sneaking up behind us, they would put grasshoppers down our blouses and roll on the ground laughing as we danced a jig of sheer terror. We were certain frogs would give us warts and ran for our very lives as the boys chased us with the slimy creatures clutched in their hands.

Nevertheless, our day finally came when Bucky passed over some mystical, male threshold and fell madly in love with Carol. Part of me felt sorry for him because I knew she was practicing her fledgling feminine wiles on him. He went skulking around like some hangdog, lovesick fool and if she looked at him or spoke to him, he would just about implode. He would suck in his breath, turn bright red and, not knowing what to say, would turn and run for the house. She, on the other hand, would smile that saucy smile, kind of like a cat licking its whiskers after a big bowl of milk, and saunter away, very pleased with herself. If I started to feel too sorry for him, I would remind myself of all the bugs and frogs he had deposited down my blouse and immediately lose all pity for him.

However, he did not have to wait long for his sweet revenge, which came in the form of a beautiful Cajun boy named Dean Allen. He was Carol's cousin from Louisiana who had come to visit for the summer, and he literally took my breath away. He had jet-black hair, luminous gray-green eyes, dark olive skin, and brilliant white teeth. When I looked at him, my stomach felt funny, my hands went clammy, and I could not catch my breath. Never before had I been at a loss for words around any male, and yet here I was, afraid I might actually swoon. I would never hear the end of it. It would be the talk of the whole ranch. I had to pull myself together. For better or worse, he seemed to feel the same way, so out of desperation, we jumped on our bikes and rode like the wind. Once we could talk to each other, we met every morning at the curb near the greenhouse and shared our most private thoughts. I was stunned to learn that he loved Jesus as much as I did and already knew he wanted to be a minister when he grew up. Even though his uncle Kenneth teased us unmercifully, saying Dean quoted Shakespeare in his sleep and cried out every night, "Oh, Rita, wherefore art thou?" we forged a bond that would last a lifetime. He went on to become a great Baptist minister and even though our paths and our doctrines often diverged, we always had a great impact on each other's spiritual journeys.

The Allens brought so much to all of our lives, but I felt I reaped the greatest benefits. Dorothy became my imago for the perfect mother because her children were the most important things in her life and she was always there for them, offering whatever sustenance they might need. She welcomed me with the same loving warmth and I basked in the glow of her praise and attention. She was the hub of that friendly, bustling household, much like Mama, and I envied their togetherness despite the fact that they had so much less than we did materially. They were the catalyst for my first conscious thoughts about why some people had so much while others had so little. I was beginning to realize that money could not buy happiness, but I was also very disturbed by the injustice of some people having great wealth while others lived in poverty.

No matter how I looked at it, I figured it must be God's fault, and this realization precipitated my first confrontation with my heavenly Father.

Angry and confused, I went to Daddy and asked, "Why are we so rich while other people are so poor? I don't think that's fair."

Daddy looked as if he could have gone a lifetime without having to hear that question. He shook his head and said, "Honey, I'm afraid I don't have a good answer for you. People have been asking that question since the beginning of time and I think we each have to find our own answer or at least, some belief that helps us live with it. I believe that if you are blessed with wealth, you have a responsibility to help those less fortunate. Someday, you will run this ranch, and I know that I can count on you to take good care of our people. They're like family and we couldn't operate this ranch without them. This is their home, too, and they depend on us to fulfill our responsibilities. Once you see more of the world, you'll know what real poverty looks like. It's very, very sad and all you can do is try to make it better and change what you can. I'm sorry I don't have a good answer for you, but I hope I've at least shown you a way to live with being rich without feeling guilty."

Daddy waited quietly while I thought about what he had said. I finally responded, "Mama says it is more blessed to give than to receive. Maybe God made us rich so we could give a lot and make things better. Thanks, Daddy. I feel a lot better. I know what to do now."

Daddy looked mystified but relieved as I kissed him before leaving on my sacred mission. Within the hour, I gave half of my clothes to Carol and I did feel blessed, at least, until Mother got hold of me. She said Dorothy had called to say she was very embarrassed that Carol had taken the clothes and that she would be returning them immediately. Looking at me sternly, Mother said that I had humiliated them and that was no way to treat friends. Using her most disappointed tone, she told me to go help Carol bring the clothes back. When I saw Carol's tear-streaked face, I felt terrible, lower than a snake's belly. I learned right then and there that this "giving thing" was a lot more complicated than I had thought. But it was not long before I got a real lesson in giving.

CHAPTER 30

Mother's Role on the Ranch

Age Nine

Since coming to the ranch, my mother had gradually taken over more and more of the duties associated with running a large ranch household. She made it a point to meet all of the ranch employees who worked at our headquarters, as well as their wives and children. She let it be known that she did not believe in rigid class barriers and that she was available if anyone had a problem. Everyone knew that was true of Daddy, but they breathed a sigh of relief knowing that he had married a woman who shared his respect for people. In time, she became the matriarchal figure people could turn to with personal, sensitive issues that were more easily shared with a woman. Mother loved babies, any kind of babies, as long as they weren't hers, and it became a tradition for all new mothers to pay her a visit. She would drop whatever she was doing, grab the baby, and after oohing and cooing for about half an hour, she would hand the new mother a hundred dollar bill and whisper, "Tuck this away and buy yourself something nice." My mother had a sincere appreciation for the relentless rigors of motherhood.

One day, Jessie, our top shop hand, came to deliver a message from his wife regarding the new gardener and his family. As Mother listened intently, I saw her Irish color begin to rise and I knew there was going to be hell to pay. Jessie was saying they had just had their twelfth child and the mother and new baby weren't doing well. Jessie's wife had gone over with some food and was appalled by the conditions in the house.

Jessie swallowed and finished by saying, "My wife said you would want to know." With tears brimming in her eyes, Mother said, "Juanita was right. Please thank her for sending me word, Jessie."

Turning to Dorothy, she said, "We've got to get over there right now. Please put together a cleaning basket and a food basket. I have no idea what we'll find there but it's best to be prepared. Meet us at the house when you've got everything together. And Rita, you're coming with me. One day, this will be your job and you might as well start learning right now."

While Jessie was getting Mother's car, she looked at me intently and said, "I want you to mind your manners. No matter what we see there, act respectful and don't show any shock. We don't want to embarrass them." As we pulled up in front of the house, I realized that it was one of the few houses on the ranch that I had never been inside. Situated as it was down a bit from the big shop where Shorty did his welding and just a little east of the catfish hole, I had passed it a thousand times but never had the occasion to go in because there hadn't been children there before. There were children here now, that was for sure. They were everywhere. A couple of the more curious children approached us cautiously as the oldest boy ran into the house to tell his mother they had visitors. In a moment he returned; looking as though it pained him to speak, he said, "My mama said she's feeling poorly and please excuse her but she's not up to company."

Looking at him tenderly, Mother said, "I know, dear. We're here to help," and marched past him as if she came here every day of her life. Jamming his hands deeper into his pockets, he looked at me with an odd mixture of defiance and wistfulness. Not knowing what else to do, I reached out my hand and said, "I'm Rita."

The boy looked at my hand as if it were a snake. He hesitated, and then, smiling self-consciously, said, "Nah, I'm all dirty," and thrust his hands back into his pockets. He was not wearing a shirt and his painfully thin body was streaked with dirt and sweat. My heart went out to him but all I could think to say was, "It must be a lot of fun having so many brothers and sisters." He looked at me in disbelief and then with a patient weariness a thirteen-year-old should not have known, he replied, "Not really."

I suddenly realized how stupid I must seem and I was grateful for the gracious way he dealt with my ignorance. Just then, I heard my mother calling, so I ran into the house but stopped short as soon as I went through the screen door. Nothing in my life had prepared me for what I saw there. I was standing in an almost bare kitchen that held only an old ice box, a small stove, and a square table situated in the middle of the room. On top of the table sat the biggest jars of peanut butter and jelly I had ever seen. There was a knife inside one of the jars and an opened loaf of bread was lying nearby. But what really stopped me in my tracks were the swarms of flies covering both jars. They would lift off briefly if a child approached to dig inside the jars, only to settle again and resume their gruesome feast.

Trying not to show any reaction, I followed my mother's voice into the living room. There was no furniture there either and I saw my mother sitting on a mattress on the floor. Lying on the mattress was a skeleton-thin woman who looked as if she could die at any moment. She appeared old and worn out, though she probably wasn't much over thirty. My mother was holding her hand and whispering to her softly as she cried quietly, not making a sound. Lying in her arms was a newborn infant too weak to even cry, and all I could think about was: How in the world am I going to keep from crying?

Hearing me enter the room, Mother turned to me and said, "Run to the house and tell Big Charles to put bedding in the hunting wagon and to come here at once. This lady is very sick and needs to go to the hospital."

Grateful to have an excuse to get out of that house, I ran like the wind, furiously wiping at the tears gushing down my cheeks. Now I knew what Daddy meant about poverty being sad.

But it was worse than sad. I felt as if the anguish would crack my chest wide open and break my heart into a million pieces. I didn't know who to be mad at or how to make the pain go away. Daddy had been wrong about one thing. I didn't have to travel far to see poverty up close and personal because it had reared its ugly head right here in our own backyard. For me, it was one of those pivotal moments that would define the person I would become just as surely as the stinging dust storms sculpted the harsh Texas terrain. I would never be able to look at our perfect world in the same way ever again.

When I reluctantly returned to their house later in the day, I found Mother talking to the gardener while an army of people cleaned, made repairs, and filled the house with furniture and appliances. The lady and her baby were going to be alright and it was gratifying to see how quickly poverty could be eradicated when people cared and took action. But years later, when I was confronted with poverty-ridden cities and countries that could not be fixed so easily, that gnawing feeling would come back to haunt me. I knew it haunted Mother, too, because later that night I saw something I had never seen before: my mother crying and seeking solace on Daddy's broad chest. She kept repeating, "How could that happen here?"

CHAPTER 31

Rubirosa and Daddy's Fall

Age Nine

As always, lessons were learned and you moved on; ranch life didn't leave much time for licking wounds. I was glad there was a real high point coming up—a polo game here at the ranch. And this wasn't going to be just any old polo game; this was going to be the granddaddy of them all. Each of my favorite people were coming in for this grand event and I could hardly wait to see them.

First, there would be the Maharajah and the Maharani of Jaipur, and I knew Aisha would be bringing me a beautiful sari. I loved playing dress-up in those luscious silks and pretending I was an Indian princess, even though I knew that life had some serious drawbacks. Because Aisha was Indian royalty, swimming in our pool was a rather elaborate ordeal because no man could see her in a swimming suit. Consequently, all of the male workers had to clear the area until she was fully clothed again. I was her appointed chaperone and I took my job very seriously.

Years later, after all of the Indian royals had been stripped of their power and possessions, Joyce sent me an article from the London newspaper about Aisha's children. They were surviving by conducting some kind of harem tent excursions into the desert and I applauded their ingenuity. Their parents had taken Mother and Daddy tiger hunting atop elephants and now they guided adventure-starved tourists through the seductive mystique of Arabian nights. If there was one thing we all learned from our parents, it was how to throw a hell of a party.

Uncle Duke would be coming, of course, and I was really looking forward to hearing about his recent movies. Tex Ritter, Rex Allen, and Slim

Pickens would probably come in early for the polo game before they performed at the rodeo next week. The Gorleys would be coming in from their Vermejo Ranch in New Mexico, and Russell Firestone would be there with some beautiful new woman. Uncle Rayworth would be playing on the opposing team, so I knew the rivalry would be intense.

Most of the top polo players in the world would play in this game, but the one that all of the ladies looked forward to seeing the most was Rubirosa. Just the sound of his name could set them all atwitter. I didn't know what all the excitement was about because he wasn't nearly as good looking as Daddy Charles or Uncle Duke. One evening, as I eavesdropped on my mother and her friends playing cards, I finally found out the secret to his charm. Aunt Norma was saying, "I heard he's dating a new heiress. Do you think he will bring her?"

"Oh, heavens no," my mother replied. "He's much too smart to bring a woman with him unless she is the new wife." In a conspiratorial whisper, Aunt Mildred said, "Well, I heard he studied with Hindu masters in order to control all of his body functions. They say he can keep an erection up to twelve hours. Can you imagine?"

They almost squealed with delight as I pondered what purpose that would serve. None of our best studs could do that, so I figured it couldn't be all that important. When I asked Daddy about it, he almost choked and after he recovered he asked, "Who on earth told you that?"

Looking a little ashamed, I replied, "Well, Aunt Mildred told the other ladies and I kind of overheard." With a twinkle in his eye, he leaned close to me and whispered, "Rubi does have a secret but it's not what the ladies think. If you promise not to tell, I'll share it with you." Wide-eyed, I nodded solemnly and crossed my heart. Looking first to see who might be listening, Daddy said, "He's not just another playboy like most people think. He's also a patriot fighting for his country's freedom. There's more to Rubi than meets the eye so don't judge him too harshly." My imagination was on fire and I begged Daddy to tell me more but he shook his head and said, "That's all I can say. Remember your promise."

Years later a book called *The Adventurers* was rumored to depict Rubi's life and I remembered Daddy's words. But then, even later, I read a lengthy article about him in *Vanity Fair* magazine and it seemed no one ever really knew Rubi. And maybe that was best, so his mystique could live on, immortalized with other legends like Don Juan and Rudolph Valentino.

The night before the game was heavenly. Lights sparkled in the trees and a band played in the cabana by the pool. Big Charles had a goat and a side of beef on the spit down at the barbecue pit. He pulled off a succulent piece of *cabrito* (goat) and a juicy slab of beef for me that more than filled my plate. Lester and Mel circulated with teriyaki sticks and *rumaki,* and I managed to grab a couple even though Mel gave me the evil eye. Juggling my contraband, I made my way to the bar, where Billy was serving drinks. Settling into one of the saddles, I asked for a Coke and prepared to watch the show.

My parent's friends were extremely entertaining and I waited with excited anticipation. Would Little Ann from the Four 6's ranch fall into the pool with her big floppy hat on? Would Daddy and Uncle Lloyd do a song and dance number wearing sombreros? Would Mother sing a torch song with the band? One never knew. That's what made it so exciting. When you had that many colorful people together, you could always count on something memorable happening.

Unfortunately, the most memorable thing that happened over that three-day period was Daddy's accident during the polo game. He and Mama Lu were racing toward the goal posts, flanked on either side by opposing players, when she suddenly stumbled over a mallet that had gotten tangled between her feet. As she went down, Daddy catapulted over her head and hit the ground hard. I saw Mother and Uncle Duke run past me toward Daddy but I stood dead still, barely able to breathe. I held my breath as I waited for either Daddy or Mama Lu to move. I knew their stillness was a really bad sign, especially for Mama Lu, because a horse's first instinct is to stand, no matter how hurt they are.

Finally, I saw Daddy make a small movement. He was talking to Mother and then, everyone turned to look at me as Daddy gave me a weak wave. I felt an explosion of air release from my lungs as I raced toward him. By the time I reached Daddy, he was up on his knees bending over Mama Lu. She lay breathing hard as Billy Skidmore patted her down for broken bones. I was afraid to touch either one of them, as I heard Uncle Rayworth tell Daddy he should be still due to probable internal injuries. Ignoring him, Daddy asked Billy if she was hurt bad. Shaking his head in wonder, Billy said, "I can't tell it if she is. We'll know more in the next twenty-four hours. Let's see if we can stand her up."

With a powerful effort, she lurched to her feet, shook her head, and began snuffling Daddy all over, the way any mare would with an injured colt. Looking up at Uncle Rayworth, Daddy laughed and said, "Looks like she doesn't trust your opinion, Doc."

Daddy grimaced with pain and lay back down so they could lift him onto the stretcher. Mama Lu was soon fit as a fiddle but after a week of tests, we were told that Daddy did have some internal problems. It turned out that the real problem was all the fluid on his belly, which was the result of the cirrhosis in his liver. One more fall could mean his death, and so, just like that, his polo days were over. Trying to make light of this devastating loss, Daddy said, "At least my last game was a rip-snorter."

He didn't fool anyone because we all knew that this edict could be a death sentence in and of itself. My heart broke for him as I tried to picture his life without polo but I had also suffered a rude awakening. The blinders of childhood were gone and my enemy had a name, *cirrhosis*, and I would do battle with that enemy until Daddy took his last breath.

Buster in his El Ranchito polo uniform

Buster astride his polo horse

Polo skirmish

El Ranchito Polo Team. *Left to right:* Buster Wharton, Jessie Smith, Billy Mayer, Billy Skidmore, and Shorty Switzer

CHAPTER 32

First Adoption Talks

Age Nine

Mama was always saying, "When it rains, it pours!" and I was beginning to understand what she meant by that. I had just almost lost Daddy and now something was up with Daddy Charles. He was coming to Vernon, something he never did. I couldn't imagine what horrific thing could force him to brave the perils of small-town West Texas life. Mother and Daddy would only say that he wanted to talk to me and would be staying at the hotel in town.

The whole thing seemed very odd to me and I anxiously waited for Charles to speak as we sat in the hotel café. He was diligently cleaning the silverware with his napkin, while his nostrils flared with slight distaste from the greasy smell of burgers on the grill. Far too gracious to offend anyone, he gave the waitress a blinding smile as she approached the table. The poor girl dropped her pen and pad and nearly fainted when he swooped down to retrieve them for her.

I really couldn't blame her. He did look just like a movie star in his signature glen plaid suit and his stunning good looks. But I was used to women falling at his feet, and I wanted her to go away so I could hear what he came to say. I was beginning to agree with Mother about one thing: All that adoring attention from other women got old real fast. I made a mental note to tell Daddy Charles to rein in that charm just a tad since he obviously didn't know how lethal he was for women. That was the unbelievable truth. He was a genuinely kind, sweet person inside an incredibly handsome outer form who just naturally dispensed love like manna from heaven. His mere presence set women on fire and I often saw the sad surprise in his eyes as he heroically tried to put those fires out without hurting anyone. Every man envied him and every woman wanted him, but no one ever knew how hard it was to be him. He walked a tightrope all the time, trying to control the impact he had on others, and the price he paid was sheer exhaustion.

Now, as I sat watching him work up the courage to tell me something I knew I didn't want to hear, my heart felt his lonely isolation. I reached out and took his hand, as he had so often done with me, and asked, "What's wrong, Daddy?"

Looking at me sadly, his green eyes began to well up and he quickly smiled and said, "You know, I don't want to do this here. Let's go up to the room."

Later, sitting on the bed, holding both of my hands in his, Charles looked directly into my eyes and said, "Buster wants to adopt you and your mother says you would like that. Is that true?"

The room began to tilt and there was a loud roaring in my ears. I was engulfed by an avalanche of emotions, and I could not have articulated any of them. I sat mutely staring at Daddy Charles, trying to think of something to say. I wanted the earth to swallow me up so I wouldn't have to play this no-win game. Who should I hurt? How could I choose between the two men I loved more than life itself? Feeling like a cornered, wild animal, I tried to think of a way out. "What would that mean exactly?" I whispered.

Trying to sound nonchalant, Charles said, "Well, Buster would become your legal father."

Dread rose up in me as I asked, "And what about you?"

"I would not legally be your father anymore," he answered quietly.

Stricken, I flung myself into his arms and cried, "I can't do that. Please don't make me. I love both you and Daddy Buster."

He held me tight and soothed me, saying, "I'm sorry, Darling. It's our fault. We never should have put you through this. We won't talk about it anymore. I'm so sorry, sweet girl."

After a few moments, I lifted a tear-stained face to ask, "Will Daddy Buster be mad at me?"

Laughing and rocking me gently, he said, "Of course not, Sweetheart. He'll understand. He loves you, no matter what. We both do. Forgive us for dragging you into our adult nonsense. Now, let's go see if we can find a hot fudge sundae in this one-horse town."

When Charles took me home, he told me to go to my room so he could talk to Mother and Daddy in private. After he left, I could hear Mother as she approached my room, her footsteps a quick staccato on the wood floors. I had long since learned how to gauge her mood by the tempo of her gait, so I prepared for the worst.

Bursting into my room, she glared at me as she hissed, "How could you hurt Buster that way? After all he has done for you! How could you betray him like that?"

Tears streamed down my face. I pleaded with her to understand. Just then, Buster came up behind her and said quietly, "Lu, that's enough. Let me talk to Rita alone."

Filled with guilt and sorrow, I stared at Daddy wide-eyed as I waited for the verdict. Looking sad, he said, "Will you forgive me, Deets? I meant to do a good thing but I didn't think about what that would do to you. I'm so sorry."

The words gushed out of me as I ran into his arms and hurriedly explained why I couldn't do the adoption. "Charles is so alone, Daddy. He doesn't have a family like we do. We're his family. I just couldn't make him be any more alone than he already is. Do you understand?"

Looking at me with tears in his eyes, he said, "Yes, I do, Sweetheart. I surely do. And I'm so grateful you got your grandmother's understanding heart." I wasn't sure what he meant by that but I knew my world was right again and that was all that mattered.

CHAPTER 33

First Solo Campout

Age Ten

As long as I could remember, I had been begging Daddy to let me spend the night at the chuck wagon with the cowboys; alas, to no avail. He always said Mother didn't think it would be appropriate and I always responded with, "But they're my friends. They would take good care of me."

But this time he smiled slyly and said, "Well, your mother doesn't think it would look right and besides, Johnny already thinks you're a little heathen."

Jumping on Daddy as if to prove the charge correct, I squealed, "I'm not a heathen!" I tickled him as hard as I could. Underneath the laughter, though, I knew what Johnny Biggs thought was a serious matter.

Mother said that Daddy and Johnny had had some words over the way I was being raised. I think the exact words Johnny allegedly used were *wild as an Indian* and *unruly*. He didn't approve of my fraternizing with the help, and since he had to drive by our house to leave the ranch at least twice a day, he got an eyeful of all the fraternizing going on. When I told Carol what he had said, she scoffed, "What would a Yankee know about wild Indians? And what does he care what you do, anyway?"

I didn't have an answer for that, and I was just about to ask Daddy that question when he smiled and said, "Well, you've worn me down. I've got a deal for you . . ."

Daddy had taught me that persistence pays off since I was knee-high to a grasshopper, and this time it was paying off in spades. As I jumped up and down with delight, he said, "Whoa, now. Don't get too excited until I tell you some of the concessions you'll have to make. Your mother is still adamant about you not staying at the chuck wagon but we could do a little test run on you camping alone. How would you feel about that?"

I pondered my decision, reluctantly letting go of my fantasies about sitting around the campfire with the cowboys, watching Leftie roll a cigarette with one hand and singing "Deep in the Heart of Texas" while Cookie the cook poured everyone a fresh cup of coffee.

Resigned, I yelped, "Yes! Yes! I want to camp alone."

"Okay, here's the deal," he said, smiling. "I will blindfold you and take you to a central location on the ranch. Once you're settled in, I'll leave and you can camp alone overnight. If you can find your way home by sunset of the next day, you can camp alone whenever you want. Have we got a deal?"

Wild with excitement, I began to mentally make a list of all the things I would need. I would have to travel light, mostly food and bedding. I thought it would be nice for Mama Lu to have a couple of apples while I enjoyed my s'mores. And Rosie was going to fry up enough chicken for Daddy and me to have a picnic before he left me alone for the night.

That evening, I lay sleepless for hours as I dreamed of all the possible adventures that lay ahead.

The next morning we rode out to a beautiful day, enjoying a comfortable silence, with Daddy occasionally throwing out reminders of things I already knew. "What do you do if you hear a rattler? What do you do if Mama Lu gets hurt? . . ."

I answered all of Daddy's questions because I knew it made him feel better, but I wasn't worried. I had waited for this chance at freedom my whole life and I was going to make the most of it. After we passed Hoot 'N Hollar Bridge, Daddy put the blindfold on me. I remember realizing that my only resistance to having my eyes covered was not being able to see all of the life buzzing around me.

After what seemed an eternity, we finally stopped and Daddy said I could remove the blindfold. As I looked around, I couldn't say for sure where I was, but Daddy just laughed and said, "Check out the sun now, and tonight you can set a course by the stars. You'll be fine. Trust your instincts. Besides, if worse comes to worse, you can always let Mama Lu lead you home." Horrified, I stood with my hands on my hips and hissed, "Never!"

After we made a fire and ate our fried chicken, I started making s'mores so we could eat them while we watched the sunset. Daddy smiled indulgently as I carefully placed the scorched marshmallows between the graham crackers and Hershey bars. Munching on his s'more, Daddy grinned and said, "You're getting to be a better cook. These are a lot tastier than those mud pies I used to eat."

Glaring at him, I said, "Very funny, Daddy."

We sat quietly watching as the big, red ball of fire sank into the heat waves on the horizon. Red, gold, and pink tendrils of wispy clouds were splashed across the bright blue sky and I thought my heart would break from the sheer beauty of it all. I looked over at Daddy, and I knew he felt the same when I saw the tears in his eyes. As the stars began to blink out, Daddy prepared to leave, gruffly throwing back at me, "Thanks for the grub. Hate to eat and run, but this is your big night. Best to be getting on with it. See you tomorrow, Squirrel."

As I watched Daddy ride off into the darkness, I suddenly felt a lump in my throat and just for a second, I wanted to call out to him, but I didn't. I stood my ground and started plotting a course like he had told me to do. Once I felt comfortable with the direction I would take in the morning, I fixed another s'more and gave Mama Lu another apple. As she contentedly crunched on her apple like an old cow chewing her cud, I began to serenade her with all of the open range songs I knew. She looked patiently bored and whinnied occasionally when her keen ears picked up a sound she couldn't identify. I put more wood on the fire and wondered if a coyote would come close like the cowboys said they did when it got really quiet. I smiled happily to myself and drifted off into a peaceful sleep, knowing that Mama Lu would stand guard.

Several times during the night, I could hear the coyotes singing nearby but none came up close to the fire. I was disappointed, but I planned to bring some raw meat to tempt them next time.

Just as the sun was coming up, I kicked dirt on the campfire embers, greedily wolfed down a biscuit with honey and fed Mama Lu. After checking the direction of the sunrise, I swung into the saddle and said, "Okay, old girl. It's just you and me."

We rode east for a while, and then some instinct made me turn north. After a couple of hours, I realized Daddy had taken me in circles while I was blindfolded because we weren't that far from Hoot 'N Hollar Bridge. We were making good time now so I thought it would be nice to wash off in the creek if there was enough water. In answer to my question, Mama Lu seemed to sense there was water nearby and quickened her pace.

As I lay in the creek, splashing the cool water over me, I felt a sense of accomplishment and I knew I had just crossed over an important threshold. I was so grateful for this chance to prove myself, and right now, what I wanted most was to see Daddy's face when I rode in, way before sunset.

Years later, Mother confessed to me that Daddy had hidden a few hundred yards away and watched over me throughout the night. Knowing I was never out of his sight didn't diminish my achievement, it only made me love him even more. He had made my dream come true, it didn't matter how he did it.

Buster in the ranch living room

CHAPTER 34

Decisions and Shopping

Age Eleven to Twelve

Life seemed to slip by like a multicolored kaleidoscope as I watched all of the adults around me trying to navigate towards some new plateau. My parents were desperately trying to fill up the hole in their lives left by the absence of polo. Daddy was suffering from the syndrome associated with retiring athletes—a fear-induced depression that screamed, "If I'm not a world champion polo player, who the hell am I?" In his eyes, polo was the only thing that distinguished him from the multitude of other rich, alcoholic playboys.

After a brutally honest self-evaluation, Daddy concluded that his other passion, hunting, was the only viable means of reinventing himself. He had always lived by the motto *When in doubt, go on safari!* Now, he desperately needed Africa to rebirth him and refresh his life as she had done so many times before. It was a logical, convenient choice because Mother's hunting skills now equaled his, and she loved Africa as much as he did. She could easily see herself in the role of "big-game hunter's wife," but she also aspired to rival any man with her courage and skill in making the kill. She was already ordering fabulous new hunting clothes from Abercrombie & Fitch and I knew she would be the best dressed woman to ever go on safari. They would be taking a photographer with them, as usual, so it was important to keep up appearances while filming the hunt and their day-to-day camp life.

There was only one small snag in all of these elaborate plans: Me. Joyce and Eddie were getting married so she couldn't take care of me. To make matters worse, Aunt Avis was going to college at Southern Methodist University so she and Mama stayed in Dallas most of the week and only came home on weekends. Thus was born the great idea that I should go to a boarding school.

Daddy had fought the notion for years, but now, even he could see the benefits. After days of frantic phone calls and skillful negotiations, my fate was sealed. Joyce would take care of me until school was out, and then Grace would come to stay with Avis, Mama, and me for the summer. When it was time for school to start, Joyce would take me to the new school and get me settled in. It seemed like a workable plan, and now I just had to select a school.

Mother and Daddy had picked out three schools for me to choose among, each one selected because of a particular asset to me. Pine Manor offered not only an excellent education but also boasted a top-notch equestrian academy. Hockaday was a good finishing school in Dallas and offered close proximity to home. Bishops was in La Jolla, California, set like a Spanish jewel against breathtaking views of the ocean. After visiting each one, I was lured by my old friend, Neptune. Naturally, I chose Bishops, to be by the sea.

Having gotten some major decisions out of the way, they all went back to their frantic gyrations of preparing Mother and Daddy for their safari, planning Joyce's wedding, and getting me ready for boarding school. As busy as Mother was, selecting my new clothes at Neiman's was not something she would entrust to another soul. So off we flew to Dallas for my initiation into one-day shopping at Neiman Marcus.

Mother had already warned Daddy and our pilot that we would not be home till close to dark, so Daddy, brilliant man that he was, opted to stay home. Upon our arrival, we were led to Mother's regular dressing suite in Ladies' Fine Clothing, where we were offered coffee, tea, or hot chocolate, accompanied by a continental breakfast sent from their world-famous restaurant, The Zodiac Room. One end of the room was filled with full-length mirrors, positioned to show off a dress from every angle. The other end of the room featured a comfortable couch, two chairs, and a coffee table that offered Coca-Colas, ice, a menu, and a phone. Racks of clothing had been preselected for me to try on, and Mother and I culled the ones we didn't like as we sipped our coffee and hot chocolate.

Then it was on to the serious business of trying on the remaining possibilities. By one o'clock we had selected the "definites," the "nos", and the "maybes," so we decided to break for lunch while the ladies worked their magic. Mother's favorite saleslady had set aside a few fabulous new arrivals for Mother to try on while we waited for our lunch to arrive from The Zodiac Room. Admiring Mother's style in a particularly daring dress, Helen shook her head and said, "I had my doubts about that one but you could make a potato sack look good." I saw the sincerity on her face and knew she must be glad to be able to say that to a customer and mean it.

After lunch, we made our final choices and then proceeded to the necessary alterations. Finally, after what seemed like hours of standing, we made our exit amid much fanfare with hugging and kissing.

On our way out, we stopped in the bakery to get Daddy an angel cake, famous for its moist, spicy flavor and its rich buttercream icing with thinly sliced almonds encrusted over its entirety. As we stood outside waiting for a cab, a cool breeze danced between the tall buildings of downtown Dallas and I thought, "This was a perfect day. This is a day I will never forget." And I never did. Mother and I had finally found something we could share, and I cherished our female bonding. I smiled as I thought to myself, "Daddy Charles is right. There might be something to this girlie-girl stuff, after all."

CHAPTER 35

Spring Roundup

Age Twelve

Learning to be a world-class shopper was nice, but something even better was coming up soon. It was spring and that meant only one thing to people on a ranch—spring roundup. It was a festive time, gathering all of the newborn calves. It was the rancher's time to reap what he had sown and everyone was in high spirits. Any kind of harvest struck a chord in us, galvanizing some primitive instinct with the promise of abundance for the year, but the roundup fulfilled a lot of different needs for everyone. Young, green cowboys, eager to prove they were up to snuff, dreamed of this opportunity. Roundup would separate the men from the boys and the youngsters knew they would be working with the best there was—seasoned, hardened cowboys with years of experience.

Roundup was a precision event that took raw skill and perfect timing executed by a team of cowboys. One would rope a calf, preferably by the back heels, and drag it to the fire where two cowboys (flankers) would throw the calf on its side to begin the process, while a fourth cowboy waited with the branding irons. Each calf was branded, vaccinated, castrated (if a bull) and earmarked with a V notch (if a heifer), and sometimes dehorned. It takes extraordinary strength and skill to hold down a calf that could weigh up to three hundred pounds and kick the stuffing out of you if you lost your grip during its introduction to hell. Top cowboys could get it all done in thirty seconds, and then throw the stunned calf to its feet and turn to reach for another one to do it all over again, and again, and again.

Timing had to be perfect on both the part of the roper and the flankers in order to keep the line moving efficiently. A bad castration could kill a calf, and that left no margin for error.

Cowboying is not for sissies; if the backbreaking work doesn't get you, the smell of burning flesh and hair will sure get your attention. Michael Pettit's book, *Riding for the Brand,* gives the best explanation and description of roundup that I've ever seen. The first time Grace came to a roundup, she warily eyed the branding irons heating up in the fire and nearly swooned when the iron made contact and sizzled on the flesh of the calf. Joyce, on the other hand, took right to it in her usual undaunted manner and learned to cook the best calf fries I ever ate.

When a calf is castrated, the sacks are kept, used as a count, and then divided up between the lucky recipients. For ranchers, calf fries are a delicacy that is only available once a year, so we made the most of it with a big cook off. We always froze a few to get us through the year, but most of them were cleaned, battered, and fried in the big, cast-iron skillet.

Daddy loved watching the faces of his unsuspecting city friends when they politely asked what they were eating and he would grin and answer, "Calf fries," and the elegant ladies would ask, "And that is what, exactly?"

"Bull testicles, my dear," he would snort, grinning even bigger, as he watched her poor, dandified husband turn green around the gills.

"A rare delicacy in these parts, much sought after, and we only share them with our special guests. Isn't that right, Lu?"

Mother, looking exasperated but amused, would say, "Please don't feel you have to eat them. They're an acquired taste, much like oysters. In fact, they do taste a bit like oysters, don't they? That's why some people call them 'mountain oysters.'"

Daddy, looking a little deflated after Mother stole his thunder, had to admit her hostess skills were flawless and would give her a wink to let her know there were no hard feelings.

I always loved watching the cowboys work, especially Eddie, but this year seemed a little different. It occurred to me that I might not be here for roundup next year, and in fact, it was the last roundup I ever saw. Grace told me she was stunned by the brutality of the whole procedure and I was trying to see it from her perspective. Still, the rancher in me said, *A cow is a cow, and this is the life of a cow.* It was a typical, practical acceptance of life on its own terms, and it had never occurred to me to question it, any more than I would question what life dished out to me.

Why was not a question country people could afford to ask, so we accepted the cards we were dealt and tried to figure out how to get out of the game alive. I figured that little calf was thinking pretty much the same thing, and as soon as he got back to his mother's warm milk, he forgot about his brush with hell. At least, that's what I would have done. Besides, I had seen other animals and people suffer a lot longer than thirty seconds and not come out of it near as well. Dorothy Allen always said, "Chicken one day and feathers the next." That's just how life was. Some good days, some bad, some you met head-on and some you hunkered down. But at least you stayed alive to fight or dance another day. It wasn't a fancy philosophy, but it made a lot of sense to a survivor.

CHAPTER 36

Summer in Dallas and Aunt Avis

Age Twelve

It was summer. Joyce was happily married and busy setting up house with Eddie on Cowboy Row. That was where the married cowboys lived and Joyce glowed with wifely pride as she settled into the nest with the other wives. It turned out that sporty, determined Joyce loved flowers so their house was a floral bouquet of varying shades of blue.

When Bucky and I asked Eddie how he liked all those flowers, he smiled with his usual good nature and said, "Well, it's peaceful." Looking somewhat conspiratorial, he leaned towards us and whispered, "It's an English thing." "Oh," we breathed, as if that explained everything.

Seeing Joyce so happy made it a lot easier to leave for Dallas, so I was eager to begin my first summer in the city. Mama, Avis, Grace, and I would spend the next two months at Avis's apartment. It was heaven spending long, leisurely days with three of my favorite people in the world. While Avis was at school, Grace and I would lounge at the pool or play checkers and Pollyanna with Mama. Grace did most of the cooking and a multitude of other things that seemed to keep her eternally busy.

That was the one thing that Joyce and Grace had in common—neither of them could remain idle. Mama always said, "Idle hands are the devil's workshop," so I knew ol' Diablo would never get his hands on either of them.

I spent hours laying in Mama's lap getting my back scratched; eventually content, I would jump up to play beautician, which entailed fixing Mama's hair and face.

She had been letting me cut and style her hair and put on her makeup since I could remember. My first attempt was disastrous, leaving her with a bloody scalp and looking like she had gotten caught in a chicken plucker, but she defended me, saying, "Oh, it'll grow back." I kept practicing, and by the time I was a teenager, she wanted me to do her hair and makeup for any special occasion. By unanimous decision, it was I who prepared her for her final journey home to meet her maker. I savored that sacred labor of love, knowing it would be the last time I would ever touch that sweet face.

On this particular rainy day, Avis's playful side was showing and she announced that she and Grace were going to dye my hair. She used a copper color on her hair, which always inspired people to say, "Your hair shines like a new penny," much to her delight, and now she was going to share that womanly art with me.

Mama was horrified, but her protests fell on deaf ears as the two younger women, amid peals of laughter, conjured over me like two brujas tending their cauldron. Never one to be left out of the fun for long, Mama finally relented and even agreed it was a beautiful color on me. I felt like a real grown-up, but mostly, I was just glad to be doing anything that Avis did because she always had some new interest that was fun and exciting. Now, in her early thirties, she was going to Southern Methodist University to get her bachelor's and master's degrees in psychology.

When Mother and my Uncle Jackie went off to college, Avis stayed home to take care of Mama. At last, her turn had come, even though she could not rid herself of the guilt she felt for dragging Mama back and forth between Vernon and Dallas. But Mama never complained because she was proud of Avis's independence and encouraged her every step of the way. Having had so little freedom in her own life, Mama wanted her girls to be able to do whatever they wanted. She would have done anything for all of her children, but Avis's interests were always a special delight to her.

During the war, like many other patriots, Avis got deeply involved with ham radios, to the point that she converted the back porch into a "ham shack" with all of the best equipment. She bought one of the first home movie cameras and proceeded to document the Judd family life, much to everyone's dismay. Nevertheless, years later, when she had the films converted to videos and distributed them as Christmas gifts to the whole family, there were not enough words to express how grateful we were for her labor of love.

After her filmmaker period, Avis raised show chinchillas and converted the garage into a temperature-controlled nursery for the persnickety little critters. It was like a meat locker in there, but we never tired of watching them bathe in their special "dust," rolling and frolicking with such joy. After she won the national championship, Avis moved on to racehorses. Mother had given her and Mama two fine mares, so after doing her homework, she began breeding them to the best studs in the area, namely, Oscar Dodsen's champion bloodline.

Even though Mama did not believe in gambling, she could not help but enjoy the "Calcutta Races," which were a slick camouflage to get around the ban on horse racing in Texas. When teased about being seen at a racetrack, she defended herself by saying, "Lu gave us those horses and it wouldn't be fair to her or the horses if we didn't let them do what they love to do."

As the horses came down the track toward the finish line, it was hard to keep our eyes on the horses because watching Mama was so much fun. You could see the war taking place within her—a war between her Baptist morality and the fun-loving girl who had been suppressed all of her life. Eyes twinkling, she would jump to her feet, self-consciously force herself to sit back down, only to jump up again, with her fist hitting the air as she whispered, "Go, girl. Go." Her sons teased her mercilessly about what the Baptists would think, but she would always reply in her demure fashion, "I don't know for sure that horse racing is a bad thing. Jesus hasn't given me an answer on that yet and until He does, I am going to support my horse."

As it turned out, she never had to make that hard decision because Avis lost interest in racing when her best, two-year-old horse shin-bucked in a race he was winning in Ruidoso, New Mexico. Seeing him blow out his leg, when he was destined to be such a champion, broke her heart. Even though she kept them all as expensive pets, she never raced again.

For a brief time, she raised Angora goats, compliments of my mother, who had passed a truck load of them and found them so adorable, she flagged the driver down and bought the whole load as a diversionary gift for Avis. Unfortunately, Angoras are considerably more delicate than regular goats, and that winter was spent maintaining heat lamps and hauling babies into the warm bathroom in Mama's house. Even though they were precious, Avis quickly had her fill of that dubious gift and moved on to bigger and better things.

In between farming, coin collecting, and the antique business, Avis started a contracting company in order to remodel the rent houses she had inherited as well as the houses she had bought to turn a profit. She was a hard taskmaster, and only one man was able to put up with her perfectionism and all that went with working for an independent woman; that man was Archie Monday. They fussed and fought like a brother and sister, but Avis always said there wasn't anything Archie couldn't do.

During the summer, when most of the boys I knew were looking for work, they would run the other way when I mentioned she had work for them, saying, "Hell, no. That woman will work you to death and it's downright embarrassing to be outdone by a woman." I knew what they were talking about because when there were no extra hands around, Avis and I unloaded truckloads of hay, stacking it in a barn that was probably 103 to 110 degrees during the heat of the summer.

Just looking at her, you would never guess that this beautiful, extremely slender young woman was such a knowledge-hungry, hard-driving entrepreneur at heart. She and Mother were as opposite as two women could be. Avis had thick, lustrous brown hair that seemed to dance in tune with her infectious enthusiasm for life. Her hazel eyes sparkled with a joyful expectation, and she could light up a room when she smiled, showering everyone with the goodness that emanated from her. Nevertheless, she had no desire to be in the limelight and was not the least bit dazzled by celebrity or wealth. She was the woman for whom the sleek, tailored clothing of the '40s was intended, and her demeanor was much like that of Katherine Hepburn and Barbara Stanwick. The contrasts in her nature seemed to give her an irresistible mystique, and therefore, my childhood was enlivened by a parade of men who came to call. They were even willing to suffer the brutal inquisition of a precocious child while they waited and waited for this woman who was always late. However, when she entered the room with her eighteen-inch waist and her long, slender legs, you could see that they would have happily waited another few hours.

My all-time favorite was her fiancé, Hamp Nailor. They had dated since she was fifteen and everyone, especially Hamp, just naturally assumed they would get married after high school. When the war came along, he became a flight instructor at Victory Air Force Base and she didn't seem to be in any big hurry to tie the knot. I could never understand her reluctance, because he was tall, dark, and handsome and won my heart by shamelessly spoiling me. He taught me how to walk by twisting my nightgown into a handle and then propelling me around the room until I grew tired or fell—no easy feat for a man six-feet-four-inches tall. He waited eight years for Avis to marry him, and I was heartbroken when he gave up and married someone else. He went on to start a crop-dusting company and became mayor of Vernon, but I just wanted him to be my uncle.

A succession of suitors followed, including another eight-year stint with Fred Smoker, a well-to-do farmer and very likeable man, but no one could hold Avis's attention for long; she remained a virgin and alone. When I asked her if she regretted never marrying, she admitted that when she dreamed she was married, she always woke up nauseated and in a cold sweat. I always thought she incorporated Mama's feelings of frustration and entrapment into her own being and thus feared marriage and losing herself above all else. Her extreme sensitivity to other people's feelings made her vulnerable to nervous overload, giving her a fragile quality despite her bigger-than-life ambitions. She remained a woman of faith, principle, morality, and charity but most of all, she is the mother of my heart. As long as I can remember, she has always been there to comfort me, protect me, or fight for me.

CHAPTER 37

Joyce and Me in California

Age Twelve

That summer awakened something in me, and I somehow knew that I was on the brink of a rite of passage as old as Time. I was changing from a child into a girl, but sadly, it would not be the ethereal metamorphosis I had envisioned. I would soon be so grateful for that summer of childish innocence because, in the blink of an eye, I was to be catapulted into the dark intrigue of the adult world. Never again would I view life through the rose-colored glasses of a child.

There was not a lot of time to contemplate that impending transition because Joyce and I were leaving for California. She had decided that we would visit San Francisco before going on to my school in La Jolla.

I had never eaten Chinese food except at the Canton Restaurant in Vernon, so I was enthralled with the authentic tastes, the vibrant colors, and the bustling noise of Chinatown. The seafood at Fisherman's Wharf and the seals on the pier were two of the highlights of the trip, but the event that would leave the most lasting impression was our narrow escape from death.

After we got settled into our oceanfront hotel, we decided to go for a swim. The water was chilly and buoyant as we swam out to deeper water, pushing over some kind of netting. We assumed it was a demarcation for small children or inexperienced swimmers. Occasionally, we stopped to rest and look at the clear blue sky, floating on our backs and letting the waves gently rock us into a relaxed reverie. Finally, Joyce said, "Come on, Ritz. Let's head in so we can get ready for dinner." As she swam toward shore with her powerful strokes, I began to realize that I was falling farther and farther behind. My arms and legs were moving but I didn't seem to be getting anywhere. I was trying to get Joyce's attention, but she was staring at something on the beach. Suddenly, she turned toward me and even at such a distance, I could see the stark terror in her eyes. But when she shouted, "Rita, swim toward me! Swim," her voice sounded calm and I took heart, thinking nothing really bad was happening. I could see a man on the beach, running back and forth along the shoreline, but Joyce's voice, increasingly urgent, demanded that I look at her and keep swimming toward the net.

My arms and legs were beginning to tire, but once again, I heard her voice yelling, "You're caught in a current. Swim parallel to the shore until you feel a break and then swim hard for the shore. You're almost there. Don't quit, Rita."

I felt like I was caught in molasses, but I could hear Joyce's voice, closer and closer, so I mustered the last ounce of strength that she had taught me every athlete can call upon in a desperate situation. Suddenly, I felt my hand hit the cable, and as I struggled to grab it, a strong, freckled hand reached across the cable and latched onto my arm, roughly pulling me across the net.

Looking shaken and on the verge of tears, she asked, "Are you alright?" We were still in the water but able to stand.

Feebly, I answered, "Just tired. What's wrong on the beach?"

Rolling me over and tucking her strong arm across my chest, she said, "We'll talk about that on the beach. Just rest. I'll take you in."

As we crawled onto the beach and lay exhausted and gasping for air, the lifeguard ran up to us and said, "Thank God you're okay." Joyce was on her feet in an instant and with her eyes drilling holes into him, she screamed, "Thank God is right. No bloody thanks to you, you coward. Why the hell didn't you help me? Isn't that your job?"

Humiliated, the lifeguard mumbled, "I'm sorry, but I'm not paid to go into shark-infested waters beyond the net. We recently had two bad shark attacks and that's why the net is up and the beach is deserted."

When her dander was up, Joyce was a sight to behold and the young man cringed as she took a step closer to him and hissed, "Then why didn't you tell me before we got in the water?"

Looking even more forlorn, he whispered, "I didn't see you."

With a disgusted snort, she gave him one last contemptuous look as she said, "You didn't see two people on a deserted beach. You're pathetic."

Turning to me, she said, "Ritzy, let's get out of here."

I knew the manager at the hotel was going to get an earful, but for my part, I was just thankful that Joyce had forced me to do all of those kicks at the side of the pool in Texas, even though I had whined, *Why do I have to do these? What good do they do*?

Oblivious to my grumbling, she would answer, "It builds up the strength in your legs. Keep kicking." She pushed me past my endurance day after day and on this particular day, that tough coaching saved my life. Like most people who have had a near-death experience, I was elated to be alive. But little did I know that something far more consequential was taking place in Africa, something that would turn our world upside down, never to be the same again.

CHAPTER 38

African Safari

Age Twelve

Mother had packed for weeks, driving everyone crazy, but poor Dorothy had caught the brunt of it as she followed Mother around with a pad and pen in case something needed to be added to the list. We all made fun of her, but list-making turned out to be one of the most valuable things Mother ever taught me, and it served me well later in life.

As much as Daddy loved safaris, I knew he dreaded this packing-frenzy phase, and he routinely ground his teeth in order to keep his mouth shut, lest he say something that would set Mother off on an emotional tirade.

The total opposite of Mother, Daddy leisurely puttered around his dressing room, creating little piles of clothing, which he would later organize in his trunk. Occasionally, Big Charles did something for him, but he did most of his own packing. He saw clothes as a functional necessity rather than one of the main events on a safari.

Perhaps he could be so comfortable in his own skin because he had nothing to prove, whereas Mother had everything to prove. In her mind, she was still running the gauntlet in her transition from small-town, country girl to sophisticated world traveler. She felt she was on trial every moment and, being accustomed to being caught on film at celebrity events, she put her clothing together like a general would gather his arsenal before a battle. She was deadly serious about her appearance and Daddy, knowing this, tried to be as patient as he could possibly be.

Even Daddy's patience wore thin as he paced back and forth, waiting for her to get ready to leave for the airport. Looking at me with a bewildered expression, he would say, "I just don't understand; it never gets any better.

She has had weeks to pack, she knew our departure date, and she is still going to make us miss our plane. She knows it takes four hours to drive to Dallas and if the traffic is bad, we won't make it. On top of that, she's going to be exhausted because she pulled an all-nighter. Will you explain that to me?"

This was a little ritual Daddy and I went through every time they traveled, so I played out my part by saying, "Daddy, you can't make sense of it. It's a girl thing." Glowering, he turned and pointed a finger at me as he said, "Promise me you will never be like this." I smiled and promised, ready to move on to my next distracting maneuver.

Suddenly, he whirled back to me and said, "That's it. I can't stand it anymore. I'm going to teach your mother a lesson. I'm leaving and she can get there the best way she can. Go tell your mother I'll hope to see her in Dallas."

Turning pale, I squeaked, "Me?" I knew you weren't supposed to shoot the messenger, but I had been hiding out for a week and I didn't want to press my luck now that salvation was so close at hand. Seeing my dejected look, he softened and said, "Okay. I'll do it myself."

I toyed with the idea of eavesdropping but decided against it because I knew I would be able to hear Mother's response just as well from a safe distance. I positioned myself in a strategic spot near the door and waited for the fireworks to begin.

Much to my surprise, I heard nothing until Daddy came striding toward me and said, "Come here and give me a kiss, Squirrel. I love you, and I'll bring you back something neat from Africa. Have a fun summer. Mama and Avis have all of our numbers."

I was so shocked that he was actually going to leave her that I could barely focus on his departure. I stood in stunned silence as he drove away, picturing the hell that awaited us all if Mother missed that plane. My thoughts reeling, I jumped as I saw her heading my way but she barely noticed me and seemed quite calm. She was too busy calling Jesse, offering him two hundred dollars if he could get her to the plane on time. God only knows how fast they drove but Jesse did even better than that; he got her there before Daddy arrived. Mother and Jesse gloated over that feat for years, but I thought two hundred dollars didn't seem like much money for risking your life. But more importantly, Daddy learned a valuable lesson: When you try to teach Mother a lesson, she not only gets mad, she gets even.

Preparing for any safari is an elaborate ordeal, but my parent's safaris were logistical nightmares because of their special needs. Since neither of them drank liquor, they had cases upon cases of Coca-Cola and ginger ale shipped to Africa with the rest of their supplies. It was hard for me to picture Mother in Africa without air-conditioning, a hairdresser, and a maid. Instead of doing without, she simply charmed the camp boys and had them falling all over themselves, competing to see who could get her blouse the most wrinkle-free and who could kill the most life-threatening bugs for her. She would bravely hunt lions, tigers, grizzlies, gorillas, rhinoceroses, and elephants, but she got weak in the knees and screamed like a little girl when faced with spiders or scorpions. As for her hair, she gave up the bouffant French Roll for the more natural look of a ponytail pulled back with a colorful scarf. How she kept her hair platinum, I'll never know, but I suspect she taught one of the camp boys to bleach her hair.

Mother was always a mysterious delight to the Africans because of her pale white skin that did not tan and her white-gold hair that glistened in the sun. She and they seemed to share an affinity of some kind, and it was always heartbreaking for her to leave behind those beloved new friends whom she had bonded with during the safari. She always said she was never happier than when she was in Africa. Something about that land spoke to her soul and only there could she drop her facade and feel free to be herself.

Africa appealed to her competitive spirit, as well, and she was determined to become a world-class hunter known for quick, clean kills. She and Daddy both felt there were far too many accounts of rich, incompetent hunters who mortally wounded Africa's magnificent animals, getting the White Hunter to finish them off or leaving them to die a lingering, painful death. Mother did not believe in being mediocre at anything, and she earned her place in The American Women's Who's Who for always taking her own shots and for being the only woman, at that time, to have killed a bongo. On this trip, she was gradually earning the respect of the White Hunter and the gun bearers as they watched her shoot every day, displaying courage, sportsmanship, and integrity.

Her chance to really prove her worth came on the day she faced down a charging rhino. She became a living legend among the aides that day, as they told and retold the story of the courageous blonde lady who stood her ground and slowly, decisively took aim and shot the rhino between the eyes. He dropped dead not fifteen feet from Mother and the White Hunter, as the gun bearers cheered from behind nearby trees. Mother later said she had never been more calm in her whole life as in that moment of the kill, and Jack, the White Hunter, turned to her, equally calm, and said, "Good shot. I knew you could do it." He had bet his life on it, and he could give no greater validation to her than that. In that moment, Mother bonded with the White Hunter in a way she had never known before and our lives were ripped apart, forever.

You would think something that gut wrenching would have made a horrible sound, reverberating all the way back to Texas, but there was no sound and we had no warning. Daddy must have sensed what had happened, but he chose to ignore it and remained in Nairobi for six weeks while Mother and Jack tracked down a bongo in the swamps of Africa. I can only surmise that Daddy was immobilized by his fear of losing her and retreated to let it run its course, in hopes that it would end on its own volition. But it did not end, and even though Mother and Daddy returned from Africa together, they were never really together again.

They both began to drink and each hid in the darkness of their failed dreams and broken hearts. I did not know for a long time what had brought this slow death into our lives, not until the movies of the hunt arrived. It was unfortunate that we had a house full of guests, which meant more witnesses to the celluloid documentary of an affair so blatant that it broke your heart to watch it. There was utter silence as we all sat spellbound, watching Mother repeatedly exclude Daddy and fawn over Jack. When I turned to look at Mother, I realized she didn't even see it, she could only see Jack and her eyes sparkled like a teenager. She didn't notice when Daddy quietly slipped out of the room, but I did, and I wanted to scream, "Turn it off! Can't you see you're killing him?" But I did not say anything, and we all continued to watch the film in much the same way you would watch a train wreck—horrified, yet, unable to turn away.

By the end of the movie, I wanted to kill my mother, but instead, I went to find Daddy. He was sitting in his dressing room, having a drink. I sniffed the glass, wrinkling my nose as I recognized the smell of vodka. Looking at him with pleading eyes, I said, "Daddy, I'm so sorry. But please don't drink. Don't leave me here alone."

Turning tear-filled eyes toward me, he said, "I guess your old dad seems pretty pathetic right now. I'm sorry about that."

Putting my arms around his neck, I said, "It's not you that looks bad, Daddy, it's her. You can divorce her and I'll stay with you."

Looking sad, he patted my back and said, "I'm not your legal father. It doesn't work like that, Honey. And besides, I still love her. I know that must seem weak to you, but I hope, someday, when you're older and you fall in love, you'll understand and forgive me." Making a feeble attempt at humor, he said, "I can't live with her and I can't live without her." I didn't know what to say, so I just kept my arms around him, holding his hand so he couldn't reach for the glass.

Years later, Dorothy Allen told me that Jack had come to the ranch in hopes of persuading Mother to leave with him. They met at her house and talked for several hours, but he left alone. Viewed through a glass darkly, you could say she stayed because Jack could not offer her what Buster could. On the other hand, you could say she stayed for Daddy and me. Who can know the inscrutable mind of a woman in love, or the primeval urges that can drive her over a forbidden precipice. Whatever her reasons, she stayed and took us all down into that black abyss with her. Poor Daddy had gone to Africa in order to save his life, but through an ironic twist of fate, he had lost it instead.

This was the beginning of his slow but sure, alcoholic suicide. Mother couldn't take all of the credit for his demise; there were others waiting in line to throw fuel on the fire and become willing accomplices in his self-destruction.

Only one good thing came out of that affair. When adoption was brought up again, we all agreed it was the right thing to do, and Buster legally adopted me when I was twelve years old. It was painful for Charles, but he did it for my sake, thinking Buster could protect me better than he could. That would turn out to be a fallacy, but we didn't know that yet. All we really knew was that our home, once filled with love and laughter, was now seething with misery and silence. It was as if a dark cloud had descended over the house and even though I hated to leave Daddy, I was grateful to escape their unhappiness during the school year.

CHAPTER 39

Bishop's School

Age Twelve to Thirteen

My first year away at school was what my grandmother Rena would have called "a broadening experience." It was as if my whole world had been turned upside down and everything seemed different. I was living by the ocean in a large town but, regrettably, confined to a very small space in a strict private school for girls.

The girls were like none I had ever met, and I felt like a child compared to them, which I suppose I really was. I marveled at their glamorous looks and their grown-up sophistication, but I was baffled by their cynical attitude about life. Most people refer to this outlook as "jaded," and I was accused of possessing that very trait in a few, short years.

My best friends were girls more like me; a little ignorant, maybe, but not scary. Beverly was my sporty, California friend and we shared a love for horses. She took me horseback riding on the beach for the first time and it was exhilarating. I could feel the joy of the horses as they splashed through the surf and whinnied to each other in their great excitement. My other good friend, Robin, was gentle and could sing like a bird. Robin's family owned beautiful public gardens in Canada and I looked forward to her parents' visits almost as much as she did. They were two of the most attractive people I had ever seen, and I had seen a few, but what intrigued me most was her father's loving devotion in the care of his wife's hair. Her long, dark hair almost reached the ground and because of the arthritis in her arms, she could no longer maintain it. Consequently, Robin's father took over the duties of washing and brushing out the long tresses until they were dry and shining. Robin and I could spend hours watching him at his labor of love and I would coax Robin into singing "Summertime" and many other favorites.

The Bishop's School for Girls presented me with an interesting paradox in many ways. A large kitchen staff, which included some of the best chefs in California, prepared all of our meals but we, the boarders, served the food at each table. We worked on rotation and I looked forward to my turn because the servers got an extra hot fudge sundae. In fact, I liked the food so much that I gained twelve pounds and left behind my thin, coltish body for a more filled-out, teenaged one. I didn't get nearly as much exercise as I was used to getting, so my days of being rapier thin were over.

The most profound gift that Bishop's had to offer me was my introduction to the Episcopal church. Since it was an Episcopalian school, we had prayer time or vespers twice a day in the chapel. The beauty of the quiet, melodious ritual was in vivid contrast to what I had been exposed to, namely the Baptist preacher screaming hellfire and damnation, and ladies rolling down the aisle amid a lot of great singing and hand-clapping at Miss Mandy's church. Even though I couldn't sing a lick, I joined the Episcopal chapel's choir and signed up for confirmation classes.

As I sang and stared in rapture at the beautiful stained-glass windows, I knew I was being introduced to another path to God and I was enthralled with this new passageway. Only in nature had I felt this sense of peace, and I was relieved to know there was a place of refuge for me in the city.

CHAPTER 40

Pigeon Shooting

Age Thirteen

The safari films had arrived while I was home for Christmas, so I didn't know what to expect when I got home for the summer. I had lived in dread the previous four months, fearing Mother would leave Daddy and take me with her.

When Daddy called, he never spoke of Mother but rather talked about Molly's puppies or about how mad at me Mama Lu was. My ears pricked up at that and I gasped, "What's she mad at me for?" After a long sigh, he said, "Well, she said you didn't bring her any carrots, sugar cubes, or ice cream when you were home at Christmas and she's mighty upset about it." All of my worries forgotten, I immersed myself in the wondrous world of sweet fantasy that Daddy always created for me. Quickly, I replied, "Daddy, please tell her I'm sorry and I'll make it up to her when I get home. I'll take her something extra special." Chuckling, Daddy said, "I'll tell her, Squirrel. She really wanted to tell you how the cow ate the cabbage, but I bet that bit of news will cheer her up."

When I finally arrived home, all seemed the same on the surface, but a dark, seething undercurrent ran below the artificial veneer. I felt like I was walking on eggshells, just waiting—for what, I didn't know, but that constant state of fear and anxiety drove me to find relief in the make-believe facade that we presented to the world. We all acted out our parts and kept the secret, but by now there were so many secrets, I hardly knew which one I was keeping at any given time.

Mother and Daddy had each chosen an avenue of escape and now we all threw ourselves into ballroom dancing and pigeon shooting. We drove down to Wichita Falls two or three times a week for lessons at the Arthur Murray dance studio. Actually, it really was something we all enjoyed, and Daddy and I got our bronze medals, while Mother got the gold medal, of course. Doing the fox trot with Daddy was one of those cherished memories that a girl never forgets, even when she is old. It was one of those exquisite father-daughter moments that brings the refrain, "You will always be Daddy's little girl, no matter how old you are."

It was fun learning to dance the waltz, fox trot, tango, swing, mambo, samba, cha-cha, and merengue, but pigeon shooting was the preoccupation that consumed most of our time, just as polo had once done. Daddy had hired the best pigeon-shooting trainer in the country, and Bill Wise came up from Laredo to coach us into readiness for the Championship of Mexico.

Pigeon shooting had originated in Mexico, but it was becoming extremely popular with the Texas hunting crowd, so almost every hunter we knew was preparing for the competition, as well. We spent a lot of time in Mexico that summer, going to most of the smaller meets in preparation for the big event.

Pepe and Jose were the two best pigeon-throwers in the world. Their art was cloaked with intriguing secrecy, so we all watched them closely, trying to solve the mystery. Although their throwing styles were quite different, they both performed the same basic movements required in pigeon throwing. Taking a pigeon in both hands, they would pass before the contestants, showing them that the bird was alive and well. Returning to the center of the ring, they would lean over, cover their hand movements, and pluck certain feathers from the wing or tail. Then, like a whirling dervish, they would spin and throw the bird high into the air. The pigeon had to be shot within the ring, so you only had a matter of seconds to get the bird in your sights and take your shot as the bird tumbled and zigzagged through the air. The plucked feathers determined what sort of erratic flight the pigeon would take, making pigeon shooting much more difficult than trap or skeet, which were reliably predictable in the direction and velocity of the clay pigeons.

Throughout the summer, I had won several of the junior divisions, but when we went to Monterrey for the national championships, I was a little intimidated because I knew the reigning champion, a sixteen-year-old Mexican girl, would be there. She was a living legend in the gun world, and three years older than me. When I met the sons of a friend of Daddy's, I accepted the drink they offered me, along with their ill-advised counsel: "It will calm you down."

It calmed me down, all right. I was barely coherent when Daddy came to get me ready for my turn. Looking at my bleary eyes, he asked, "What's wrong? Are you sick?"

One of the brothers, snickering, said, "I think she's just a little drunk, sir."

"Drunk?" Daddy exploded. "She doesn't even drink!"

In unison, the brothers cowered and whispered, "Sorry sir," as Daddy glared at them with paternal rage. "Do you know what you've done? You may have cost her the championship. This shot will determine who wins. She's only thirteen, for crying out loud. What were you thinking?"

Looking shocked, the boys squeaked, "We didn't know. We thought she was older."

Bringing his attention back to me, Daddy asked, "And you. What do you have to say for yourself?"

Feeling sick and ashamed, I said, "I'm sorry, Daddy." Looking somewhat mollified, he said, "Well, let's see if we can fix this. Let's get you some water and coffee."

After plying me with all of the home remedies he could think of, he asked Kirk Johnson, a good friend of his, to accompany me to the line. Daddy was afraid his own agitation would distract me and make me even more nervous.

Kirk turned out to be the perfect choice because his calm guidance enabled me to do the impossible, and I made a new, if somewhat unusual, friend that day. As we walked to the line, he quietly ran through the checklist with me, saying, "Focus on the bird, Rita. Nothing else exists. Take your time. Aim and squeeze. It's as easy as falling off a log. You've done it a thousand times. Now, go get 'em, girl. Make your Daddy proud."

He knew just the right things to say to me, and after I called out, *Listo!* (ready), I zeroed in on the bird and pulled the trigger. I heard the sympathetic groan of the crowd, I saw the bird still flying and severely rattled, I mentally chastised myself, "Too quick. You rushed the shot."

Suddenly, I heard Kirk's calm voice, "It's okay. Forget that. Focus. Take your time. Squeeze the trigger." Almost in slow motion, my mind's eye took in the bird, the shot, and the roar of the crowd. The pigeon had fallen dead one inch inside the ring and I was the new champion of Mexico. Just like that.

My darkest moment had been transformed into my greatest achievement, but I wasn't really sure I deserved it. Because I had been drinking, I couldn't be positive it wasn't just luck. Daddy was pumping Kirk's hand and saying, "Now, that dog will hunt. I owe you one, buddy."

As Daddy whirled me in the air, congratulating me, we both turned toward a loud voice that was drowning out all of the other sounds. The sixteen-year-old former champion was being berated by her father for having lost, and he backhanded her to the ground as I watched in horror. I felt, as much as saw, my father lunge forward, but Kirk grabbed his arm, saying, "No, Buster. Stay out of it. We're in Mexico, as their guests. You know it will dishonor him if you interfere with his family."

Daddy grudgingly relaxed and said, "He's dishonored himself, but you're right. Let's go get that trophy, Deets."

The Mexican people, always so warm and gracious, tried to make the occasion as special as possible for me. When they called my name to come up and accept the trophy, the announcer misspoke my name on purpose, and said, "Will Miss Rita Hayworth, I mean, Miss Rita Wharton, please come up and accept this trophy as the new Champion of Mexico."

As I accepted my trophy, a large, cylindrical, silver bowl, about the size of a large watermelon, all I could think about was that poor girl being slapped and humiliated by her father. It was ironic that the greatest achievement in my short shooting career was to be the catalyst for the death of my competitive spirit. I suddenly realized that in all competition there is a loser, and I wasn't particularly thrilled with being the winner at someone else's expense. I still believed in competition with oneself, the pursuit of excellence, but my competitive edge was gone, never to return. No sport, no game, could mean so much that I would betray my humanity or sacrifice my honor in order to win.

CHAPTER 41

Mother Drinks

Age Thirteen

A large group of our friends took us out for a celebration dinner and most of the conversation was about the spectacular shot I had made. They told the story and retold it, each from a slightly different perspective, and I was wishing I could feel better about that shot and more comfortable with all this attention. Some speculated about who might challenge me next year, but I didn't want to think about that so I concentrated on the food.

Many people, especially Texans, confuse Tex-Mex—a greasy and chili-based fare—with authentic Mexican cuisine. Mexican chefs magically transform chicken, beef, goat, and seafood into culinary delights that tantalize the taste buds. Surely, no culture has ever rivaled Mexico in its extensive and creative use of the lowly lime.

My mouth was beginning to water just thinking about the *cabrito* turning on the spit, and I eagerly looked forward to the rich, savory meat nestled in a warm flour tortilla and covered with guacamole, refried beans, jalapenos, and just a splash of lime.

Suddenly, I heard my name being called. Reluctantly, I dragged myself back from my culinary reverie. Mother was saying she had ordered me a celebration drink; after all, if I could shoot with the big boys, I should drink with them too.

At first, I thought she was kidding and declined, saying, "No thanks. I have a Coke." But Mother, in a slightly louder voice now, said, "Oh, but I insist. And you have to drink the first one down in one swallow. Isn't that right, everybody?"

Something in my mother's tone alerted me to a new, unknown danger, and I quickly looked to Daddy for guidance through this unfamiliar minefield. He was looking at Mother with a pained expression, and after slowly wiping his mouth, said, "I think we've all had enough liquor for one day. Besides, Rita doesn't drink, do you, Honey?" Polite chuckles filled the air, homage to my earlier drinking escapade, and embarrassed to the core, I replied, "No, sir. I don't."

Mother was not to be thwarted that easily, and as they set an enormous glass in front of me, she said, "Drink up. That's a Scorpion, and I know how you love gardenias."

Feeling sick from the fumes coming from the drink, I looked at Daddy once again, hoping to be rescued. He did not fail me. Standing up and walking over to Kirk, he quietly asked, "Would you mind taking Rita back to the hotel, and I'll have your food sent over. I need to take care of this."

Kirk, gracious as ever, said, "Of course. I understand perfectly." As he escorted me out of the restaurant, I could hear Mother's voice, loud and shrill, shouting, "You come back here, young lady! I'm talking to you . . . "

Kirk did not falter or speak a word until we were safe in the taxi. Turning toward him with tear-filled eyes, I asked, "What did I do? What's wrong with Mother?" Looking distressed and uncomfortable, Kirk said, "You didn't do anything, honey. Your dad will explain everything when he gets back to the hotel. I bet you're starving, I am. What did you order?"

Trying not to cry, I muttered, *Cabrito*. I had forgotten about my food and my stomach was screaming in protest as we pulled up to the hotel.

Daddy arrived within the hour, and running to him, I asked, "Did I do something? What's wrong with Mother?"

Looking weary and sad, he led me to the couch and once we were settled, he said, "You didn't do anything wrong. Your mother is simply drunk."

Stupefied, I parroted back, "Drunk? But Mother doesn't drink." Frowning, Daddy said, "She does now."

With the direct bluntness of a child, I asked, "Why?"

Pondering my question for a while, he finally said, "I don't know for sure. Maybe because she's unhappy."

Frightened and baffled, I blurted out, "She acted like she didn't even know me or like she hated me. I've never seen anyone act like that just because they were drinking."

Daddy frowned again, trying to find the right words. He said, "Deets, liquor doesn't mix well with some people's chemistry, and it makes them mean."

Still confused, I said, "But you never get mean."

Smiling ruefully, he said, "Well, no, liquor doesn't affect me that way but maybe I would drink less if it did."

At that moment, Mother let herself into the room and immediately began yelling at me. I sat motionless, a deer caught in the headlights, and wondered who this woman was. My mother had always treated me with polite indifference, but now she was on the attack. It would be years before I realized what had happened that day. She had seen me in a new light, and I was not just her daughter anymore, but rather, young female competition. Puberty, that mystical rite of passage that I had so yearned for, had severed my relationship with my mother, not to be healed for many years to come.

Daddy, fearing the situation would get out of hand, said, "Go to your room, Rita, and lock the door behind you." I quickly did as I was told and, standing breathless on the other side of the locked door, I listened to the bile that spewed out of my mother's mouth. It broke my heart to hear the things she said and I didn't know how Daddy could stand it.

Finally, I heard a tap-tap at the door and Daddy's voice, saying, "It's me, Deets. Let me in." I opened the door and as Daddy slipped in, I saw some flying object whizzing through the air toward the door as I slammed it shut. Terrified, I grabbed Daddy and held on for dear life, as Mother mounted one assault after another on the door that stood between us.

Finally, after what seemed like an eternity, there was silence. In my numb state of mind, I barely noticed. As Daddy tucked me into bed, he whispered, "Everything's okay. I'm going to sleep in here with you so there is nothing to worry about. She'll sleep now. And tomorrow she won't remember any of this, so we just won't say anything about it, okay?"

Mutely, I nodded in agreement, as I thought to myself, "But I'll remember it. Forever."

What an easy way out—just don't remember anything, no matter what you do. And the bonus for her was that with no memory, there was no guilt. The events of the day kept flashing through my mind and I gnawed on them like an old dog with a bone. I sighed and thought to myself,

“Another secret to keep.” I wondered how many we could keep before they started to crush us. But like any good player in a dysfunctional family, I kept the secrets. One thing had changed, though. Mother and I were officially at war now, and poor Daddy just tried to keep out of the crossfire.

When I was older, I was able to view her actions from a much broader and more sympathetic perspective, and I understood why she did the things she did. Like all of us, she did the best she could with the hand she was dealt. In the end, we made our peace and celebrated the journey.

CHAPTER 42

First Year at Hockaday

Age Thirteen to Fourteen

It was decided that I should go to school closer to home, so in the fall I began classes at the Hockaday School for Girls in Dallas, Texas. I loved that first year at Hockaday because it was still located at the original site on Greenville Avenue. The old building had character and a homey feel that made being away from home easier. Its finest asset, however, was its location. We were only a few blocks from the neighborhood shopping area, which consisted of many small shops and restaurants lining both sides of the street for two or three blocks. It was a lovely little neighborhood village that I found comfortable and not as intimidating as the downtown area.

In return for good behavior, we were allowed to walk down there in small groups for an hour or two. Aside from trolling for treats or toiletries, our primary destination was the movie theater. We rarely got to see a movie, due to our small amount of allotted time, but we gathered around the movie posters and gushed over our favorite stars. The school did take us to see *Gone with the Wind* when it was rereleased, but only because it was thought to be an accurate depiction of the Civil War, which meant, of course, the Southern perspective. I had always loved movies, but that epic masterpiece made me a devotee for life. Being a history buff, I was thrilled by the fact that movies allowed me to go back in time in order to see and feel the essence of that historical period.

That first year at Hockaday, I was an exemplary student because I loved to learn and the school provided me with rich material in the curriculum they offered. Learning was like some exotic aphrodisiac that both intoxicated me and broadened my world in ways I had never dreamed of. Unfortunately, life had more important lessons in store for me, like getting to know Death on a first name basis.

My education began with Daddy Charles's unexpected call, saying he would like to see me after school. I thought it would be just another pleasant visit, like so many others, now that we were in such close proximity, so I informed the school and alerted my classmates to his imminent arrival. My friends always liked a little prep time before he arrived so they could primp and look their best for him. They would line up like little ducklings on the stairs and each, in turn, would greet him with, "Good afternoon, Mr. Link. It's lovely to see you."

After we had walked past and entered the parlor, I smiled to myself as I pictured them swooning and falling in a heap on the stairs as they argued about which movie star he most resembled. Looking up and really seeing him for the first time since his arrival, I saw a look on his face that I had never seen before, one I didn't know how to interpret. I could feel the fear that crept into my stomach trying to eat its way through as I stared at him, unable to decipher the look of sadness mixed with resignation that clouded his face. Clearing his throat and lacing his long fingers together in an outward stretch, he finally started to speak.

I knew that gesture was reserved for gearing up to something unpleasant that he would rather not address, so I was prepared for anything, or so I thought. "Darling," he began, "I have to go in for a little surgery next week. I'm sure it's nothing, just a little mole on my back they want to remove. I don't want to worry you, but these kinds of things make you realize that there are no guarantees in life, and if there are things that need to be said, you should say them before it's too late. There are some things I want you to know so you won't ever have to wonder, and I'll be happy to answer any questions you might have."

Hesitating, he stared at his entwined fingers as I recalled all of the times those hands had acted out the children's rhyme, "Here's the church, here's the steeple, open the doors and here are the people." I felt a lump rise up in my throat as I waited. Looking at me in a very grave manner, he finally asked, "Is your mother drinking again?"

Shocked, I gasped and asked, "How did you know?"

With a mixture of sadness and anger, he replied, "The last time I spoke to Buster, there was something in his voice, something he wasn't telling me. I knew he would tell me anything that pertained to you so I deduced it must concern your mother. Have you seen her drunk?"

Almost ashamed, I whispered, "Yes."

With a stricken look on his face, he crossed the space between us and enfolded me in his arms, saying, "Oh, my darling. I am so sorry." After a moment, he pulled back and looking at me intently, said, "I had hoped she would never drink again and you would never have to see that. Are you alright?"

Feeling relieved but a little guilty, I answered, "I'm fine. It was a little scary, but Daddy Buster took care of me. It's supposed to be a secret. You won't tell, will you, Daddy?"

Taken aback, he reassured me by saying, "Of course not, Darling. I only brought it up because I wanted you to know that is why your mother and I got a divorce. Don't get me wrong, I wasn't a very good husband and she had a lot of legitimate complaints, but I couldn't take her drinking and the violence that came with it. I began to fear for my life the night I woke up to find her standing over me with a lamp poised to strike me in the head. Your mother is a wonderful woman, Rita, but a woman who shouldn't drink. Promise me you will never underestimate her, because she is lethal when she's drinking and I'm not sure Buster is any match for her. He loves her too much. Watch your back, Darling, and call me if you need me, day or night."

As Charles and I embraced in sad farewell, I thought of my mother, for the first time, as the "Fatal Flower."

CHAPTER 43

Death

Age Fourteen to Fifteen

Growing up on a ranch you see a lot of death, but it is usually of the animal variety.

When an animal dies, there are no bitter feuds or messy litigations that ricochet down through the generations. There is only peace and a sense of the natural order of all living things. The death of an animal brings sorrow, too, but a bittersweet sorrow made fragrant by sweet memories.

I was to learn that when a human dies, invisible tendrils from past grievances weave their way among the survivors and can threaten to strangle the very lifeblood from an entire family. I first experienced human death when Mammy Waggoner died at the ripe old age of 103. She was Daddy's grandmother, and, for all practical purposes, had raised him instead of her globe-trotting daughter, Electra Waggoner. Daddy was only sixteen when his mother died, so Mammy became his surrogate mother. She lived in Fort Worth, and Daddy went to visit her whenever he was there on business.

Mother and I went with him at least three or four times a year, and I always looked forward to those visits. She was in her nineties when I met her and barely stood four-and-one-half feet tall on the tiniest feet I had ever seen on a grown-up. Terribly bent and frail, she walked with a cane and used an elevator chair on her stairs. Nevertheless, she dyed her hair red until she was one hundred years old, even turning us away once when we arrived unannounced and her hair had not been colored. She was sharp as a tack until she died, and you could still glimpse the young girl in her piercing blue eyes as she cackled and clapped her arthritis-ravaged hands in delight.

She liked me to sit at her feet on a petit-point stool and tell her everything that had happened since I saw her last. While I entertained her, I curiously studied the tracks of time on her face and body. Her skin was dry, like parchment paper, with deep, soft folds, her earlobes were the longest I had ever seen, her chin occasionally sported an overlooked long hair and, most embarrassing for her, she drooled slightly. She was, still and always, ever the elegant Victorian lady. She always kept a delicate handkerchief tucked in her hand and dabbed the spittle away every few seconds. I found her infinitely interesting and she, in turn, referred to me as "the little old lady" because of my solemn curiosity and obvious pleasure in her company. She found it oddly amusing that I did not get bored like the other children who came to visit, yet I could not imagine how anyone could get bored in her house. Opulent treasures filled her home, and you could easily see where her daughter, Electra, had inherited her exquisite taste and love of collecting fine art.

When she had gathered sufficient news, she always wanted me to play the piano for her and had even gotten her beautiful, Chinese red, hand-painted grand piano tuned just for me. At the end of every visit, she would gesture around the room and say, "Look around, now. See if there is anything you want when I am gone. Check to see if anyone's name is on it and if there's not, put your name on it." She kept perfectly cut little pieces of paper to use as name tags, and upon her persistent urging, I had put my name on the piano and the foot stool I always sat on.

Even though she asked the question time after time, I never wanted anything else. Mother politely declined as a rule, and Daddy never put his name on a single piece of paper, saying it would make him too sad. In response to his reticence, she would smile indulgently and say, "That's all right, Son. I know the things you should have and I've put your name on them."

The last time we saw her, perhaps acting on a premonition, she tearfully insisted that Mother take a clock that had belonged to Daddy's mother, Electra. Daddy watched silently as the two women exchanged tearful farewells, and then he stooped to wrap his strong arms around his little bird of a grandmother, careful not to hurt her fragile bones. She beamed at him through her tears and patted his cheek, saying "Good boy. You're a good boy." Tearing up himself, Daddy kissed her on the cheek and said, "I love you, Mammy. We'll see you when we get back from Africa."

After giving her one last hug, he practically bolted for the door, leaving Mother and me behind. Stunned, my mother turned to apologize, but Mammy waved her hand and said, "It's okay. He doesn't like me to see him cry. Never has. Just give him a minute. Did I tell you about the first time they tried to put him in military school? I think he was eleven or twelve. He beat them home and came running to me to save him." She had told us that story but I never grew tired of hearing about Daddy's escapades because he never spoke of his childhood, except to tell me a big falderal about being a girl when he was little. He said he had kissed his elbow and magically turned into a boy, and I nearly dislocated my arms trying to duplicate that feat.

As I grew older, it occurred to me that I had never heard him speak of his mother, except the time a schoolmate had cut a wide gash in his mother's black leather-and-silver side saddle. Daddy was more angry over that than when I wrecked his brand new car, saying, "Some things can be replaced, others can't. Because that was my mother's saddle, it has sentimental value and there is nothing more valuable than that."

Unfortunately, Mammy's foreboding turned out to be valid, and she died while Mother and Daddy were in Africa. That safari, so full of promise, became the precipitating event that began a long line of betrayals that would plague him until he took his last breath. Already devastated by his wife's disloyalty and his grandmother's death, he arrived home to find that his cousin, Electra Biggs, had removed all of Mammy's possessions from her house and distributed them throughout the family. Even though the nametag ritual was common knowledge, she said she had found nothing with our names on it. As a token gesture, she sent over some tea towels that had belonged to Mammy and I wept for him as I watched him lovingly stroke the towels as he sat alone in the dark. That was the day he knew he was at war with his own family.

CHAPTER 44

A Family in Crisis

Age Fifteen

My second year at Hockaday began in a new, modern building off of Forest Lane. There was hardly anything around us except for a housing subdivision to the south and open pastures to the north and west. A long, glass walkway connected the main school building to the dormitories and everyone said it was a modern marvel, but I preferred the old building. Nevertheless, I didn't have time to give a lot of thought to trivial matters because of all the turmoil going on in my family.

My mother's brother, Uncle Sam, had developed lung cancer after years of chain smoking and was in the hospital in Dallas. Mama and Avis had taken an apartment across from Baylor Hospital in order to be near him and I often spent the weekends with them. Uncle Sam was Mama's first-born and she did not intend to give him up without a fight. She was devastated by the thought of one of her children dying before her, and looking tired and old, she would shake her head and say, "It's just not natural."

As we waited for the cancer to make its final journey through his brain, we had to rally for yet another crisis with the youngest of Mama's brood, Uncle Jackie. He was all good looks and charm with a killer smile, but unfortunately, he had been spoiled rotten by a passel of women who couldn't say no to him. He was more like a brother to me than an uncle and I adored him in spite of his black sheep status. He was meant to be the doctor in the family, but alcohol ended that dream, and he drifted from one scheme to another, lost and aimless, like so many boys without a strong father figure. His two older brothers, Sam and Roy, had married in their teens and began farming, so they had no time for a much younger brother. Consequently, they bequeathed him to the women, which was probably his undoing since a pattern of dependency on women began that would be the curse of his life. His wife, Shirley, had finally given up on him and taken their daughter, Linda, back to Odessa in order to make a new life for herself. The loss of the only woman he ever truly loved was the final blow to his already damaged self-esteem and afforded him the perfect excuse to imbibe even more of the family's drug of choice.

Like Mother, he was a terror when he drank and that made for a lot of scuffles and unpleasant incidents. By the time I was in college, almost every bar in Dallas had my phone number as the emergency number to call when he got too out of control or passed out. When I asked why they kept letting him come back, they replied, "Oh, he's a prince of a guy. Everyone loves him. And his lions are a real added attraction."

Uncle Jackie loved animals and lived with two lions that were the crux of the problem we were facing now. Avis had received a call saying the lions had destroyed his apartment and that the smell of cat urine made it uninhabitable. Because I could handle Uncle Jackie better than anyone else when he was drinking, Mama and Avis accompanied me to assess the damages.

Even I was stunned by the deplorable living conditions, and this was one time I was not amused because I could see the terrible toll it was taking on Mama, already exhausted from her deathbed vigil for Uncle Sam. She stared at the mess in bewildered amazement, asking herself, I'm sure, what she had done wrong and why her baby had ended up like this.

I never knew how that fiasco was resolved because I had more consequential things to worry about. They had removed the mole from Charles's back but his condition turned out to be more serious than he had thought. He had ignored the persistent itching, and like most people, kept putting off going to the doctor. In this case, time was his worst enemy and they had to remove a circle of tissue, eight inches in diameter, around the mole, but there still seemed to be some concern. When I questioned him about the prognosis, he was always evasive and deliberately vague. He had lost weight, which he could ill afford, and I was worried that the situation was far more ominous than he was letting on. As it turned out, I was right.

CHAPTER 45

Charles Dies

Age Fifteen

My first indication of the seriousness of the situation came with Aunt Elizabeth's call, informing me that Daddy was back in the hospital. She was vague about why he was there, and I did not find out he was dying until I saw him the next day. His olive skin had turned ashen and the hospital gown hung on his shrunken frame. I couldn't believe the change in him since I had seen him just two weeks ago, but I would soon learn that they didn't call melanoma "the galloping cancer" for nothing.

Seeing the horror on my face, he quipped, "Does your old dad look that bad?" Recovering as quickly as I could and ashamed of my thoughtlessness, I rushed to kiss him and hold his hand. I fought back tears as waves of fear engulfed me. He sensed my distress, and looking at his girlfriend, said, "Dena, why don't you grab a bite to eat, Hon." She hugged me on her way out and I was glad Daddy had her there.

She was a good woman, working and raising her children on her own, and yet she still found the time to take care of him. I knew she really loved him for him, not his reputation or his good looks, just him. When I asked him why he didn't marry her, he laughed and said, "Oh, I'm done with all that. Dena knows that. It never worked out very well for me and I'd hate to ruin a good thing."

A grimace crossed his face as he pushed the button for the nurse and he said, "Darling, let them give me a shot so we can talk."

After his injection, he seemed more relaxed and, taking my hand, he said, "Sorry about that. I hate like hell to have to tell you this but it looks like I won't be leaving here, Darling. The cancer has gone to my stomach, so this will be my last stop. I'm here so they can make me more comfortable until it's over. I would give anything not to have to tell you this. I'm so sorry, Darling."

Gripping his hand tight, I asked, "Isn't there anything they can do?"

Looking resigned, he said, "I'm afraid not, my sweet girl. Also, I'm told it will get pretty grim near the end so maybe we should plan for you to miss that part. I really don't want you to remember me that way. Do you understand?"

As the tears finally spilled out, I sobbed, "Yes. I do. But we're not there yet, are we?"

Folding me in his arms, he said, "No, darling girl, we're not. Let's just make the most of the time we have left and I'll let you know when we're there."

I nodded, "Yes," into his shoulder and held on tight, trying to memorize every detail of him to keep tucked away in my heart for when he was gone. It was not long before I received the dreaded call, saying, "We are there."

It was ironic timing since Buster had just entered the hospital a few days before with a bad case of jaundice. Cirrhosis-related, it indicated more liver failure and the doctors were running tests to determine the extent of the damage. Nevertheless, I couldn't allow myself to dwell on the morbid possibilities concerning Buster right then: I could only deal with losing one father at a time.

When I entered the room and saw Daddy's pain-ravaged body and the death mask that had replaced his beautiful face, I did what I swore I wouldn't do. Throwing myself into his arms, I sobbed and sobbed, as he gently stroked my head, saying, "There, there, Darling. It'll be all right. I'm lucky. I've got connections upstairs. Isn't that right? You'll put in a good word for me with your buddy Jesus, won't you?"

I knew he was just trying to cheer me up because he had never expressed any spiritual beliefs and I had never asked because I suspected he was not a religious man. Nevertheless, he had always respected my beliefs without judgment or ridicule, even though he had taken some serious heat from other people about my odd notions. Whether he was religious or not wasn't important, because I knew God loved him no matter what.

As usual, Charles had known the perfect thing to say and I did feel better knowing Jesus would be waiting for him. My biggest concern was that Daddy might be bored in heaven; if it was anything like people described, it might be a pretty dull place for a man like Charles.

Pulling back and looking at me tenderly, he said, "I want you to know that you have been the jewel of my life, and I will love you forever. Forgive me for not being a better father and know that I am so very proud of you. Maybe you turned out so well in spite of me and Buster, but I'd like to think we can take a little credit. You know, you are the best thing either of us has ever done. Thank you for that, my angel. Now, I don't want you to be sad when I'm gone, just remember all the good times. And have a hellacious party in my honor and make a toast to me. I'll be watching. You're going to have to run along now, Darling. They need to give me a shot."

As we stared into each other's eyes, knowing it was for the last time, something broke in my heart and I thought I might die of grief. He grimaced as the pain shot through him again and I turned to leave. At the door, I looked back once more and saw him bite down on a washcloth to keep from screaming.

Seeing my sweet, gentle father suffer like that was more than I could take, so I did what I had always done. I ran to my other father. When I climbed up on the bed beside Buster and wept into his chest, he held me close and patted my back, not saying a word.

Finally, able to speak, I whispered, "He's dying, Daddy. His suffering is horrible. I don't know what to do."

After a moment, he said, "Well, you could go to Neiman's and buy him a pair of white silk pajamas. These damned hospital gowns don't do much for your morale. And get him some of that horrid caviar he's so fond of."

Solemnly, I replied, "He's so sick he can't eat anything and I don't know if he even cares what he's wearing."

Daddy snorted, saying, "Charles always cares about what he's wearing. He's the biggest dandy I've ever known and I don't want him dying in a hospital gown. A good-looking rake like that deserves to go out in style. Now, you run along to Neiman's while I wheel on down to pay my respects."

A nurse pushed Buster's wheelchair down to Charles's room and the only thing I heard about that visit were the first words they spoke before Dena and Aunt Elizabeth left to give them some privacy. Buster, clutching Charles hand, said, "Ain't this a bitch. I never figured you'd go before me, seeing as how you've always taken such damn good care of yourself."

Charles, smiling weakly, whispered, "There's no justice." I would have given anything to be privy to their conversation but no one will ever know what else was said in that room and I suppose that's as it should be.

Buster left the hospital the next day. Aunt Elizabeth said Charles rallied when he heard a plane going over, saying, "I guess that's Lu and Bus headed back to the ranch. I wish I could have gone with them." He died the next day, and my emotions ricocheted between relief and anguish as I tried to come to terms with losing him.

His funeral was held two days later, giving Rena, his mother, time to fly in from California. She had advanced Alzheimer's and kept calling me Charlie as she continually asked, "What are we doing here?" In this instance, I thought her illness was a merciful blessing so she wouldn't have to suffer the way Mama had over Uncle Sam.

The whole affair was the most surreal thing I had ever experienced, and I was terrified that hysterical giggles would erupt from my mouth at any moment. The sight of Daddy's body in the casket nearly put me over the edge and I gasped in horror as I tried to back out the door.

Because he was famous for his dazzling smile, Aunt Elizabeth had instructed the mortician to make him smile for his last appearance to his adoring public. The result was ghastly. The smile looked more like a grimace and he was a dead ringer for Satan, smiling up from hell. I wanted to slap her for that and I thought, "Poor Daddy. He can't escape the control of women, even in death." Equally bizarre, his dark hair had turned white and I cringed to think what excruciating pain could have caused that.

All of his former wives, with the exception of my mother, who felt she couldn't leave Buster unattended, showed up for the spectacle, looking like they had just stepped off of a Neiman Marcus runway. From their svelte, black suits and sheaths to their large-brimmed, black hats with gauzy dramatic veils, they were perfectly dressed for this high-toned Dallas event. They kept hovering around me, saying, "My God, you are the spitting image of Charles."

Continuing to gush as she sniffled into her hanky, another wife said, "What a wonderful man he was," as another added under her breath, ". . . and such a good lover, too."

Suddenly, I saw the humor in it all and as I struggled not to laugh, I thought, "Daddy must be loving this." I think that was the day I decided it was better to laugh than to cry.

CHAPTER 46

Dealing with Depression

Age Fifteen

After Charles died, I became very despondent and my attitude took a turn for the worse. Death, like a thief in the night, had stolen my joy and I was no longer excited about learning. All I could think about was getting home to Daddy. I had already lost one father and I was terrified I was going to lose Buster, too. His health was very fragile and I was afraid this latest family feud was going to be the death of him.

Whenever we talked, I begged him to let me come home but he always refused, saying my education was the most important thing. The world did not seem like a safe place anymore and I didn't care about my education. I could feel myself spiraling down into some dark abyss but I didn't know whom to turn to for help. I didn't want to burden Daddy with my problems, because he had his own fish to fry with the Biggs family and E. Paul, and all of their squabbling over the ranch business.

Mother was more and more preoccupied with Daddy's health, but at least her drinking had leveled off to the occasional, terrifying binge. Mama was severely depressed over Uncle Sam's death and often lapsed into long, melancholy silences. Avis was heroically trying to finish her master's degree while dealing with Uncle Jackie's drunken escapades.

In school, we were put through atom bomb drills in case of an attack from the Soviet Union or Cuba, as if hiding under a desk could save you in a nuclear war. They only succeeded in scaring us to death.

The Baptist church I attended every Sunday offered little in the way of spiritual support because the minister was too busy laying a guilt trip on us for not giving more money. After six weeks of money-related tongue-lashings, I snapped and threw a handful of pennies down the aisle. Shocked, my classmates began to giggle uncontrollably, until the minister finally stopped the sermon and said, "If the young ladies from Hockaday cannot conduct themselves properly, they may be excused from the church." We happily made our escape and fell on the lawn outside, doubled over with laughter. However, when I tried to explain that I felt cheated of spiritual nourishment, going so far as to compare that church to the money-changers in the Temple, the powers-that-be did not understand and were definitely not amused.

In Hockaday's defense, schools in those days were not expected to raise children for overworked or disinterested parents, and definitely not required to provide therapy or nurturing. You were either a good kid, which meant conforming to the clone norm, or you were labeled a "problem child," such as myself.

I did have serious problems, but no one seemed to understand or care. Consequently, I began to distance from my reality, seeking refuge in my own private dream world. I had the same dream, day after day, night after night, and could easily slide into any part of that dream at will. After school, I ran back to my room and quickly went to sleep in order to escape my worries and fears.

Finally, help arrived but from a very unexpected source. I became friends with Mary Sanger, a day student who was the exact antithesis of me. She was studious and singularly responsible for her age, setting a standard of excellence for all of her schoolmates. She was class president, as well as captain of the soccer team, not to mention her myriad other activities. I couldn't imagine why she would want to be friends with me, but I was grateful someone had seen my pain and reached out. She was a true friend, always defending me, but her greatest gift to me was her family. She dragged me home, like some wounded bird, knowing her mother and father would welcome me to the nest and try to heal me.

I had known some remarkable people in my life, but no one like Morton and Hortense Sanger. Their inviting, two-story house, nestled on an acre across from the "pink wall," was like a sacred hideaway, lined with shelves and shelves of great books that were not merely for decoration like in so many wealthy homes. Being avid readers, they initiated lively and sometimes heated family discussions about the latest books they had read or world events that threatened to annihilate us on a daily basis. They didn't talk about people or parties, they spoke of ideas and great deeds and helped give birth to the social activist lying dormant in me. I never joined a march or stood in a picket line without thinking of them. Their hearts were as big as their intellects, making them dedicated participants in community service.

Hortense was instrumental in establishing Hope Cottage, an unwed mothers' home for young girls and led the community in numerous other charitable endeavors. Even though the Sangers were Jewish, they were not orthodox, so Hortense always had a beautiful ham or turkey in the fridge. Her refrigerator was the kind that made you want to pull up a chair and sit a spell, so you could graze from one delicacy to the next.

The day I met Hortense, her natural maternal instincts took over and, without blinking an eye, she said, "Are you hungry? Do you want some pie? Now, sit down here at the table and tell me all about yourself. What's it like growing up on a ranch? I've never been on a ranch."

As she easily rattled on, I began to feel all warm and cozy, like I had just sidled up next to a warm stove. Mary rolled her eyes and said, "I'll be upstairs." I could see that this was not the first time she had brought some wounded critter home, and I was so grateful that these kind people were broad-minded enough to see past my West Texas twang and country ways. The fact that I was a gentile did not seem to matter in the least and I frequently went to Temple with them.

Mary was going through her experimental, atheist phase and the rabbi would always say, "Would that you could get Mary back to Temple." In this safe atmosphere, I began to explore my Jewish roots, as a follower of Jesus. It was comforting, like coming home, to read the words that Jesus had read in the Torah and once again, I discovered another dimension of God. Unlike most Protestant churches, Temple was open throughout the day and I often took advantage of the peace and beauty to be found there. The rabbi would pass by, pat me on the shoulder and say, "You know I'm always here if you need me." I suspected Hortense had told him about me, but he never crowded me, giving me all the space I needed, as if he was afraid I would spook like some wild thing.

For years, even after I left Hockaday, I returned to that safe haven like a wayward homing pigeon. Sometimes arriving in the middle of the night, I would stand beneath their bedroom window and yell, “Hortense!” Sticking her head out and nodding toward the door, she would always let me in and ask, “Are you hungry? Tell me about it.”

Thank God for angels like the Sangers who are willing to inconvenience themselves in order to save a child from falling into the darkness.

CHAPTER 47

Dating

Age Fifteen

There was one other bright spot in my life, and that was being allowed to date. Mother had always said I couldn't date until I was sixteen, but for some reason she relented and allowed me to go out on Friday and Saturday nights that summer.

I met my first boyfriend right out of the chute and quickly moved on to going steady, much to Daddy's dismay. "Why don't you date around, see what else is out there?" he would plead, but I staunchly held to my guns and said, with some prophetic knowing, "I'm not a dating kind of gal."

And so I wasn't, and never would be. Gary was the perfect combination for me, a little on the wild side but very religious. He was a star football player for the Vernon Lions, loved to drag race his shiny, '57 red-and-white Chevy, and most important of all, he had the same coloring as Charles—black hair and luminous, green eyes.

Barbara Berry and I were the only girls allowed to drag with the boys out on Moonshine Road because we had fast cars and no fear. Daddy had given me a '58 salmon-colored Thunderbird that was built for speed and I knew how to drive it. Gary and I spent a lot of time courting in his car until his mother said she worried about us parking on lonely roads. After that, we "visited" in Gary's room and even though it was a little odd at first, his mother knew I was a good girl because she did his wash. Gary, like any good Baptist boy, had informed me that we would not have sex until we were married. He intoned, in a very solemn voice, "Bad girls do and good girls don't."

Wide-eyed, I nodded in agreement, as this seventeen-year-old boy shared his vast wisdom with me. Daddy didn't have much use for the Baptist Church, so I thought it might soften him up a little if he knew Gary's views on sex. I could tell I had put Daddy between a rock and a hard place because he would rather chew his own arm off than admit there was anything good about the Baptist doctrines. They had picketed us for years, just outside the front gate, for our heathen ways, namely, having polo games and pigeon shoots on Sunday.

At breakfast on Sunday mornings, Daddy and I sat in tense silence as he tried to get through the meal without making some rude comment about the Baptists. Finally, unable to contain himself, he would throw his napkin down and sputter, "I thought I raised you to think for yourself. Do you believe all that folderol about it being a sin to dance or play cards on Sunday? Damn bunch of hypocrites is what they are . . . drunk at the country club on Saturday night and trying to pray their way into heaven on Sunday morning. Not to mention, judging their neighbors while they're at it. It's the biggest bunch of malarkey I've ever heard. I never raised you to be a hypocrite so tell me how you can go to that church when I know you don't believe in their doctrines?"

This was the first disagreement Daddy and I had ever had, but I wasn't going to back down. Looking him square in the eyes, I said, "Gary's parents aren't hypocrites. They're wonderful people. And besides, Jesus is there and I like the singing." Daddy stared at me hard, opening and closing his mouth like a big catfish as he tried to think of a rebuttal, but since he couldn't he simply closed his mouth and ferociously attacked his blueberries and cereal.

As I got up to leave, I leaned over his back and wrapped my arms around his neck, whispering, "Don't worry, Daddy. I'm still a heathen at heart." In spite of being somewhat mollified, he blustered, "And just see to it that you stay that way. I think Jesus would be with me on this." Laughing, I stroked the few remaining hairs on his head and said, "You're probably right, Daddy." As I left the room, I heard him muttering to himself, "I know I am."

As time went by, I found out there was a double standard for boys and girls regarding sex and I didn't think it was one bit fair. We were expected to stay chaste virgins while our boyfriends took advantage of some unfortunate bad girl or headed south to Mexico. When I complained to Gary that it didn't seem right for him to be having sex with someone else when he loved me, he quickly pointed out the error in my thinking by saying, "But you're going to be my wife. You have to be pure when we say our vows."

Looking puzzled, I asked, "And what about you? Why don't you have to be pure?" Without even blinking an eye, he replied, "Because I'm a guy."

Searching his eyes, I could see he really believed that, and as a scream threatened to erupt from my mouth, I said, instead, "That is the stupidest thing I have ever heard."

He blinked and opened his mouth, but I was already out the door. Later, he apologized and said it would be all right with him if I wanted to do it, but I had lost interest. Since Daddy didn't handle those kinds of questions too well, I asked Mama what I should do. After a long pause, she answered, "Do whatever you wouldn't be ashamed of doing in front of Jesus." That seemed like a sensible answer to me. The truth be told, I knew I would be embarrassed so it just wasn't my time yet.

Unfortunately, Gary and I had other issues that became apparent when he joined me for skeet and trap shooting. After several rounds, Gary had missed several clay pigeons, while I had missed none. Quick to notice his change in mood, I tried to placate him by saying, "I practice every day. You don't."

Nothing I said did any good, so I resorted to an age-old remedy. I began to miss my shots on purpose, despite the lethal glares from Daddy, and Gary's mood miraculously improved. The whole scenario was very disturbing to me, and we parted with a new awkwardness between us. After dinner, Daddy said he wanted to talk to me. Something in my bones told me we were going to talk about Gary.

Daddy's opening line was, "I'm a little concerned about your relationship with Gary." This did not surprise me and I immediately went on the offensive. Even I could hear the defiance in my voice as I retorted, "Is it because he's not rich? You always said we should never judge anyone by how much money they have."

Looking a little hurt, Daddy said, "It has nothing to do with that. I'm sure his parents are lovely people and it is my understanding that your mother has instructed the servants that all of our cleaning go to their business from now on."

Somewhat appeased, I said, "Well, that's great. So what are you worried about?"

Rubbing his hands together as he stared at the floor between his knees, he finally said, "Deets, for better or worse, Charles and I raised you to be a free spirit with a mind of your own. We loved the way you turned out, but your mother may not have been entirely wrong when she said it could cause problems with boys your own age. They're trying to become men and their egos are fragile. A girl like you can be a real threat to their self-esteem. Do you understand what I mean?"

Feeling a little sad, I replied, "You mean like when I was out-shooting Gary and he didn't like it?"

Looking a little sad himself, Daddy said softly, "Yes, Deets. Just like that."

Thinking for a moment, I said, "I bet you think I shouldn't have missed those birds on purpose."

With sympathetic eyes, Daddy said, "I want you to be with a boy that wouldn't want you to do that—someone who, even if he's not your equal in all things, could allow you to be the best you can be, without any resentment—someone comfortable in his own skin. Perhaps Charles and I were wrong to impose our design on you and I'm sorry if it causes you grief."

Reaching out to take Daddy's hand, I said, "You didn't force anything on me. You just let me be who I am. I love you both for that. And I'll find a boy who can put up with me, Daddy, just you wait and see."

Smiling, Daddy said, "I'm sure you will, Squirrel. And one other thing I wanted to mention while we're on the subject. Don't ever marry a spoiled, rich kid like me. All I've ever done is blow what I was given on wine, women, and song, ruining my health, to boot. You can't imagine how small I feel when I walk into a room full of educated or self-made men. Those are real men, Deets. The trouble with us rich boys is we never made the money in the first place, so if we lost it, we wouldn't have a clue how to get it back. A poor guy, on the other hand, is hungry and he can make it again and again, if he has to. Honey, I don't care if you marry a ditch digger, as long as he wants to be the best damn ditch digger in the world and loves you more than anything in life."

Smiling though the tears, I said, "I won't forget, Daddy, and I know there's gotta be someone out there for me, no matter how different I am. Miss Mandy says there's a lid for every pot."

In spite of the bravado I used to reassure Daddy, a dark fear lurked in my heart: I would end up like both of my fathers, missing someone I never met.

CHAPTER 48

My Hero

Age Fifteen

That summer did a lot to pull me out of the doldrums because I spent a lot of time with Daddy at Lake Kemp. He made me a wooden flatboat that he christened *The Scootin' Fool*, and I practiced maneuvering that boat for hours at a time. I was in training for the new ski boat I was getting for Christmas and I could hardly wait to show it to my skiing buddies at Possum Kingdom Lake.

This boat was special because it had no propeller and was much safer for kids to drive in case they got careless. Aside from occasional squabbles about Daddy's drinking, vodka cleverly disguised in his grape soda, that summer was just about perfect.

If I wasn't with Daddy or Gary, I spent a lot of time with my cousin, Helen Biggs. We had grown up together on the ranch, going to each other's parties, but we had never really been close until we attended Hockaday together. She was dating a good friend of Gary's so we double-dated and always had plenty to talk about. Since we were both stuck out in the sticks, it was handy for her to drive the three miles over to my house. It was better for her to visit me because her house had to be very quiet while her mother sculpted in her studio during the day and her father had his quiet time in the evenings.

Helen, who usually appeared so sedate and in control, could get absolutely rowdy around me, which only confirmed her father's opinion of me, I'm sure. Nevertheless, it was fun to see her cut loose and enjoy herself as we lurched around the pastures in the Green Goose.

One beautiful summer day, she drove up in her mother's new black Buick and announced we were going joy riding in her car today. Eyeing the sleek, low-slung beauty, I said, "I don't think this car was made for rough pastures, Helen."

Laughing, Helen said, "Don't be silly. This is a Buick. It can do anything, and besides, it's named after my mother. See there, 'Electra.' That gives it extra protection."

Giving in, I shrugged and said, "Okay, it's your funeral."

As we sped around the pasture, throwing up clouds of dirt as we dug doughnuts in the red sand, we suddenly found ourselves launched into the air, only to come down a few seconds later with a bone-jarring thud. Stunned and shaken, we looked at each other with an awakening horror. We were still alive but we might not be for long if her mother's car was damaged.

As we circled the car, I said, "Well, she looks pretty good to have just sailed off a ten-foot cliff, but she's gonna need new shoes, for sure."

Bug-eyed, Helen squealed, "Whaaaaat?"

I clarified my meaning by saying, "Tires. Rims, too, I'll bet."

Almost swooning with fear, Helen wailed, "Where am I going to get tires?"

After pondering that question, I said, "Daddy will know what to do."

Almost in tears, Helen exploded, "No. No. Won't he tell my father?"

Grinning, I said, "Not if we ask him not to."

Suddenly hopeful, she asked, "Really?"

"Really," I said. "Now let's get started walking home."

Once we got home, I presented Daddy with our sad plight as Helen stood beside me, looking pitiful and crying softly. Ever a soft touch, Daddy frowned and said, "I can get the tires but I'm a little worried about the safety of the car after a jolt like that."

Helen, looking as if she might expire at any moment, pleaded, "Please, Uncle Buster. My father will kill me."

Looking at her thoughtfully, Daddy finally said, "Okay. I'm going to send Jesse down to Wichita Falls for the tires while they pull the car out of the ravine, but on one condition: You will take the car into the dealer right away for a thorough checkup to make sure there is no serious damage. Have we got a bargain?"

Helen nodded an adamant *Yes* as Daddy shook her hand to seal the deal.

Turning to me, he said, "You need to call her mother and say she's going to stay for dinner or some such thing. Give me time to get this done."

True to his word, Daddy got the new tires and even had the car washed in order to cover our sandy tracks. As Helen drove off into the evening, I felt so proud I thought I might burst. My Daddy had saved the day and gone up about a hundred notches in my eyes. He might be at war with Helen's parents, but he refused to let children be part of the collateral damage.

CHAPTER 49

Hard Choices

Age Fifteen

That summer, I tucked away each treasured memory with Daddy, burning it into my brain so I would never forget. Now, I knew he could be gone in a heartbeat and I wanted to savor every moment while I still had him with me.

At the end of summer, I was thrilled when he said he wanted us to go for a little ride the next day. He rarely rode anymore, saying he preferred not to ride at all rather than ride like an old lady. I was envisioning a beautiful morning on horseback with Daddy when I stopped short, realizing he had called me Rita. He hardly ever called me by my real name and that usually meant we were going to have a Come-to-Jesus talk. I quickly did a mental checklist, but I could not think of anything that would necessitate such a serious discussion.

The next day, as we relaxed in our saddles, gazing out over the ranch from a little rise, Daddy finally lifted his hand and spread it across the horizon, saying, "Someday, this won't be a real, working ranch anymore. Big ranches will be a thing of the past. I guess we've outlived our usefulness in this modern age. Ranches will be run like corporations, all about the profit and nothing about the land or the people. God help me, but I'm almost glad I won't live to see it."

After a long pause, he continued, "But you will, and that's what I'm worried about. I'm sorry to burden you with this but we've got to make some hard decisions and I can't put it off any longer. I know you're aware of the problems between the Biggses and me. Unfortunately, it looks like we're not going to be able to resolve our differences and will be going to court soon. You need to be aware of what you'll be facing if something happens to me."

Looking old and sad, Daddy said, "They're going to come after you, Deets, and there's not a damn thing I can do about it except try to prepare you and protect you on as many fronts as I can. First, when this lawsuit is settled and the Estate pays me what they owe me, you'll have a nice little nest egg to get you by, in case things go south with the ranch. Now, I know you're not gonna like what I have to say next, but we might as well pin our ears back and get her done. The Biggses will come after you, for sure, but Bucky will be your biggest threat."

Stunned, I snapped, "Bucky would never do that. You underestimate him, Daddy."

Quiet for a moment, Daddy continued in a weary voice, "Left to his own devices, maybe not, but his mother will, and you can bet on it. The only way I can stop her, for sure, is to disown Bucky."

I gasped in shock and said, "You wouldn't. It would kill Bucky."

Shaking his head sadly, Daddy said, "I'm afraid you endow Bucky with a lot more love for me than he actually has. I've never been able to get close to him, his mother saw to that, and he's never cared about the ranch. I hate to be the one to break your heart, but if you're going to survive, you have to accept that he is his mother's son and he will take the ranch from you. I've never lied to you, Squirrel, and I'm not going to start now. These are hard things I'm having to say to you, but you must be prepared for whatever they throw at you. And, you've got to be realistic, Rita. Wishing it won't make it so. Not even with your brother."

Feeling as if someone had just driven a stake through my heart, I reflected on everything Daddy had said. I knew he would never lie to me but it was desperately hard to let go of my childhood fantasies of Bucky and me running the ranch together.

Finally, as the cold grip of reality took hold of me, I asked, "Why would the Biggses want to take my part of the ranch?"

Thinking for a moment, Daddy said, "Johnny and I have been at odds for some time about how to run the ranch. He's a businessman, it's all about the numbers with him, and he sees me as a stumbling block to making this ranch a successful, corporate model. When Electra first married him, I thought we would make a great team, what with his business sense and my knowledge of the land and people. Sadly, it didn't work out that way. I think the combination of his business frustrations and his lack of respect for me kindled a powerful hatred. Who knows, maybe that old story about how the ranch originally got divided up has something to do with it, too. I don't know why, for sure, but I'm afraid you're guilty by association and he knows I've trained you in my way of thinking on how to run the ranch. You'll be a threat to his corporate plan, whereas Bucky and his mother never cared for the ranch and would probably sell out for a decent price. It's a process of elimination, Deets. Remember your survival training and how I always told you to take out your biggest threat first, and then work your way down to the least? That's the tactic they'll use on you so be ready for it."

After carefully considering what Daddy had said, I asked, "So why would disowning Bucky help me? They can't stand Bucky or his mother. They wouldn't even let him go to Helen's and Electra's parties when we were little."

Looking thoughtful, Daddy said, "If Bucky turns on you, you'll be fighting on two fronts and he could be useful to them as a diversion. Believe me, they'll figure out a way to use him. Besides, I've always found that greed can make for strange bedfellows. Disowning Bucky would eliminate your biggest threat and would be the most sensible thing to do in any attempt to whittle down the danger for you when I'm gone. I know this is a lot to take in and I'm sorry I've made such a mess of things but I feel it's urgent that we act now."

Feeling heavy-hearted, I asked, "Can I think about it tonight and let you know tomorrow?"

Daddy's face mirrored his sympathy as he replied, "I think that's only fair since I just sprang this on you. We'll talk tomorrow, but for now, let's just enjoy our ride or Mama Lu's going to be mad at us."

After a very long night, I prepared myself to give Daddy my answer. I didn't know if he would be happy or sad, but I knew he would respect my decision. As we sat at the breakfast table, watching the birds outside, I quietly said, "You can't disown Bucky, Daddy. It just wouldn't be right. You accepted him as your son and he is my brother, no matter who his mother is. I'm sorry y'all didn't get closer because you would know he's a very decent person. Whatever comes, Bucky and I will face it together. I'm not going to give up on him."

I watched a mixture of emotions flicker across Daddy's face and then, as a look of resignation took their place, my teary-eyed father said, "I'm afraid your heart will be your downfall, but I've never been more proud of you. I just hope your brother lives up to your expectations."

CHAPTER 50

Expelled

Age Sixteen

LaRita had never consented to Bucky living with us but she finally agreed to let him attend Culver Military Academy in Indiana. Bucky and I commiserated with each other by phone but in reality, we both knew we were better off where we were. He was struggling with academics while I wrestled with my wild streak, which threatened to get me into a lot of trouble. Not serious things, just normal things like smoking in my room.

Somehow, my room had been designated the sophomore smoking lounge and my classmates frequently popped in to have a smoke. On one such occasion, our housemother barged into my room and accused me of smoking. I had not been smoking, but my friend hiding in the closet was, so I had no qualms about denying her charge.

Outraged, she asked if I thought she was an idiot. "No, ma'am," I replied, as I contemplated just admitting to the charge and being done with it.

"I smell smoke," she bellowed, "so someone was smoking." As she waited for me to give her an answer, I knew I should just admit it, but something inside me wouldn't let me do it.

After she stormed out of the room, my friend came out of the closet and apologized for not coming out and owning up to it. Her father was having financial problems and had recently had a heart attack. She was afraid his health couldn't withstand the shock if she got suspended or expelled. I could relate to that so I told her not to worry about it, but I had made a powerful enemy that day, one that would come back to haunt me.

I also cheated on my guest list, but then, everyone did that. My most serious infraction of the rules was sneaking out to see Gary. He and Helen's boyfriend, Dick, would drive in from Vernon and park in the alley on the other side of the school fence. Helen and I would sneak out of a side door and meet them at our designated spot. We were always careful to get back before dawn, and by some miracle, we were never caught.

Ironically, it was not this serious offense that eventually got me expelled from Hockaday. It was simply a comedy of errors—those strange mishaps that have no explanation—that ended my sojourn at the school. A classmate from Wichita Falls was expecting her boyfriend the next weekend and he was bringing a friend. Knowing I had a boyfriend, she asked if I would go out with them just to make a foursome. I agreed and instructed her to give him the name of a boy on my approved list who rarely came to the school.

Everything went like clockwork until we went to a party and my friend started chugging drinks. One of the problems with girls' schools is that they make you do everything to excess when you get out because you know that it will be a while before you get out again. With my family history, I had little interest in liquor so I sipped on one glass of wine all evening.

When it was time to leave, we realized my friend was so drunk she could not walk or talk. Horrified, I turned to her boyfriend and said, "I'll never get her past the front desk like this. What are we going to do?"

Taking charge, his friend said, "We'll get her some coffee and walk her until she can go in," which is precisely what we did. We only had an hour before curfew so I poured coffee down her while the boys walked her between them, around and around an empty lot. Finally, we ran out of time and had to take our chances. With our arms around each other's waist, we walked into the brightly lit glass building and managed to get past the front desk without suspicion. We were almost home free when my friend began to laugh hysterically, whispering in a loud voice "We did it."

Just then, our housemother walked out into the hall as I was trying to get her back on her feet. Marching over to us, she bellowed, "What is the meaning of this? Are you drunk?" I quickly answered, "No, ma'am," just as my friend said, "No, ma'am," with a long slur, followed by a giggle. Our housemother's eyes narrowed as she said, "Go to your rooms. I'll be in to talk to each of you."

I knew I was not one of her favorites so I steeled myself for what was to come. She arrived shortly and glaring at me, she asked, "Have you been drinking?"

It did not occur to me to lie, so I replied, "I had one glass of wine, but I'm not drunk." Still glaring at me, she hissed, "If you had not led that poor, innocent girl astray, I would have recommended expulsion for you, but since you got her involved, I will settle for suspension. Shame on you for being such a bad influence."

If the situation had not been so serious, I would have fallen off the bed laughing, but instead, my mouth fell open, and then I quietly closed it. I was fully aware of my reputation as a rule breaker, so I said nothing to defend myself. As Miss Mandy always said, "Sometimes you've got to know when to cut bait and leave well enough alone." This was one of those times, so I took my suspension and went home, where I wanted to be anyway.

Still, it was not all roses at home. Mother was so annoyed she could barely look at me and when she finally did, she said, "I don't know what this will do to your chances of being invited to make your debut at the best balls, not to mention college." Looking to Daddy for support, she said, "Isn't that right, Buster?"

Daddy, trying very hard not to step in those pies, grunted some noncommittal answer and hoped for the best. I could not keep my mouth shut and I blurted out, "I don't want to make my debut. A debutante is nothing but a glorified cow, sold to the highest bidder for the sake of a mutually satisfying merger. And have you seen those guys? They're all a bunch of geeks that get their nails done more often than I do. No offense, Daddy."

Looking amused, Daddy said, "None taken." In spite of being a real outdoorsman, Daddy indulged himself with a few city luxuries such as facials, massages, steam baths, and manicures. His nails were always perfect, with a clear coat of protective nail polish which, oddly enough, seemed to fit right in with his country gentleman wardrobe, put together from all over the world.

Distracted, I came back to the conversation just as Mother was saying, "I don't know what we're going to do with you, Rita. Buster, I warned you she was going to end up wild as a march hare. We'll be lucky to get her through school."

In a conciliatory voice, Daddy said, "Well, she's got a point about debutante balls. I've gone to a million of them and they're bloody boring." With a wink in my direction, he added, "But it would be worth it to dance the father-daughter dance with you, Squirrel."

Looking over at my mother, he said, "We don't have to decide anything right now, Pooty, we've got lots of time." Whenever Daddy called her Pooty, I knew he was trying very hard to appease her, so I discreetly shut my mouth and resumed eating. I often wondered how Daddy came up with his nicknames for people. I could see no logical connection between the names and the people, but it was an honor to be given such a nickname because it meant you were special to Daddy.

What I thought was going to be a brief holiday turned into something altogether different. Two days before I was to return to school, we got a call saying the headmistress wanted us to come back a day early and meet with her. I assumed it would be a pep talk on changing my wicked ways, so I was stunned when Ms. Reynolds said, "Now, let's go over the incident once more and see if we have all the facts straight."

Mother looked as puzzled as I did as she began to recount the chain of events. When she mentioned my date, she used his real name and I nearly fell out of my chair. I frantically thought to myself, "How could she know that?"

Looking steadily at me, she asked, "Is that the real name of the boy you went out with, Rita?" Trying to swallow in spite of the dryness of my mouth, I gulped and replied, "Yes, ma'am."

With a steely tone in her voice, my housemother joined the interrogation, saying, "So you lied about the boy's name and went out with someone who is not on your approved list?" Feeling my breath quicken, I whispered, "Yes, ma'am."

Gathering herself up, she asked, "And why did you do that?"

Meeting her eyes, I answered, "Because my parents were out of town and I couldn't reach them."

Looking like the cat that ate the canary, she said, "I'm afraid that is not a satisfactory excuse and I must insist that you be expelled."

I thought my mother might faint, but Ms. Reynolds interceded and, directing a look of reproach at my housemother, she said, "If you don't mind, I would like to address Rita and Mrs. Wharton."

Mother recovered her composure and began speaking to Ms. Reynolds. "Surely, you don't mean you would expel a girl for such a silly infraction. We are frequently out of the country and it would be impossible to reach us every time Rita makes a new friend. Her father and I trust her judgment regarding friends and I will be happy to add the boy's name to her list."

Unable to contain herself, and looking as if she had just sucked on a persimmon, my housemother snapped, "I assure you, Mrs. Wharton, it is not a silly infraction. And, in conjunction with the drinking incident . . ."

Her voice trailed off as my mother rose to the occasion and in a steady voice said, "And I can assure you my daughter does not drink so I would like to hear the specifics of this drinking incident."

Assuming her most formidable posture, my housemother snarled, "My decision remains firm."

As Ms. Reynolds tried to intercede, my mother stood up and with brown eyes flashing, said, "I see. Since you felt it necessary to play this little cat and mouse game, we naturally did not come prepared to clean out Rita's room. I will send someone tomorrow to get her things. I trust that meets with your approval."

Before my housemother could respond, Ms. Reynolds broke in and said to her in an icy voice, "Would you please wait outside?"

Turning to us, Ms. Reynolds said, "This was handled very badly. Please accept my apology. We had to have another interview because the accusation was made by a student and we had to determine if it was true."

I could see the sincere regret in her eyes and I was sorry I had let her down. She was the only person at Hockaday who really believed in me and disappointing her was my one regret.

With a sad look of resignation, Ms. Reynolds continued, "I'm afraid I must proceed with the expulsion even though it pains me greatly. I have high hopes for Rita. She's an exceptional child, as you well know, and I expect great things of her. I'm just sorry I won't get to see it. Rita, you will find the right school for you, a school that can appreciate your unique character, and then, you will show them what you're made of. Mrs. Wharton, you can count on a very positive recommendation from me to whatever school you choose."

As we left the room, my housemother was standing outside the door and smiled in her simpering manner as she said, "I'm terribly sorry about this, but I hope you learned something, Rita."

I was gratified to see the sickening smile leave her face as my mother leaned toward her and hissed, "And so you should be. Shame on you! By jeopardizing a child's education over nonsense, you've done something far worse than Rita did. She's just a child but you should know better. We'll find a school where the emphasis is on education rather than pumping out little debutante brats. Good day, madam."

My mother always took up for the underdog, but I was still impressed by her fierce defense on my behalf. Everything had happened so fast, my head was spinning as Mother took my hand and said, "Let's go, Rita."

A cluster of girls waited for us at the top of the stairs so Mother said she would call us a taxi while I said my goodbyes. Turning to my friends as they all chorused, "What happened?" I said, "I was expelled."

In one breath, they all gushed, "No!" and looked at Helen. With all eyes on her, Helen said, "I didn't think they would expel you. I had to tell. You went out with my roommate's ex-boyfriend, and she was furious even though I told her you weren't interested in him. She said she would tell if I didn't. As Hall President, it was my responsibility to tell. I had to do it. I'm sorry."

As I stood in shock, trying to absorb this new betrayal, I suddenly felt free—free of all the rules, free of the mean girls who took such pleasure in humiliating those weaker than themselves, and free of the nouveau riche snobs who looked down on everyone to make themselves feel bigger. I was not clone material and I was proud of it.

As for Helen, I felt sorry for her, more than anything, and I turned to her and said, "Don't worry about it. I wanted to go home anyway."

As we left the building, I pondered the most important lesson I had learned at Hockaday. It's not what you do that matters, it's the way you do it. And, if you're willing to lie and to tell people what they want to hear, you can get away with anything. I just was not willing to play the game.

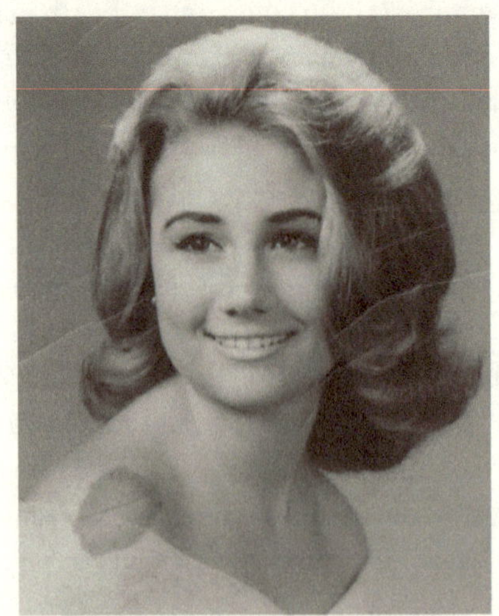

Rita at sixteen

Bucky, Rita's stepbrother, in his Culver military uniform

CHAPTER 51

Pearls of Wisdom

Age Sixteen

Even though Daddy tried very hard to play the appropriately stern disciplinarian, he was secretly delighted to have me home. Mother marched me up to his dressing room, giving him all the gory details of my expulsion, and said, "Talk to her. Explain to her that this is serious, even if those people are idiots."

He looked properly solemn as he reassured her that he would handle it. After Mother left the room, Daddy broke into a grin like a ten-year-old kid and asked, "So, how was it? I remember when I got thrown out of Princeton for running a roulette wheel. It was humiliating. Are you alright?"

Thinking for a moment, I said, "Yeah, I'm fine. It was pretty humiliating at first, but you should have seen Mother. She could have gone bear hunting with a switch, the way she stood up to that old biddy. I was so proud of her. But then, I found out Helen was the one who told on me." I was quiet for a while.

Daddy finally asked, "How do you feel about that?"

Looking up at him, I said, "Sad. But I'm not mad at her."

Smiling, Daddy said, "That's my girl. Never judge anyone until you've walked a mile in their moccasins." Suddenly, his face lit up and he said, "The pigeon shoot in Laredo is next week. You got home just in time. Now, let's have that talk I promised your mother."

With all the signs of the youngster gone, Daddy began to share his life wisdom with me, that wisdom that comes from the school of hard knocks, and in so doing, he imprinted the love of knowledge on my brain. I had always loved to learn, but his words on that day rekindled the desire into something akin to a sacred mission for the Holy Grail. The most valuable kernel of truth he wished to impart that day was to get an education, but all of his words were burned into my memory, never to be forgotten. "Time passes, whether you're accomplishing anything or not, so make it time well spent. Thieves can steal your possessions, including your land, but no one can ever take your education away. It will always be an asset to you, even if you don't realize its purpose for years to come. You will always feel like a success if you're contributing something to the world and mankind. Always share your knowledge, your money, and your compassion with those less fortunate."

So many pearls of wisdom in such a short period of time, but then, our lives seemed to be on fast-forward in those days, like a runaway horse that no one could stop. I wanted things to slow down so I could enjoy being sixteen and stop obsessing over Daddy's health and what the future might hold for all of us.

Gary and I were having problems, too, so he was not the happy distraction I had hoped he would be. In all fairness to him, my family was just way too dysfunctional for a normal person to comprehend. He saw everything in black-and-white and good or bad, while I saw everything as mostly gray, with some obscure lines between good and bad. Where some would look at my life and family as jaded, I simply saw imperfect beings trying to function at their best in spite of their emotional wounds. My independence and my family were testing Gary's endurance to the breaking point, so neither of us was devastated when he took an out-of-town job for the summer. Plus, I was going to be busy with summer school at Midwestern University in Wichita Falls in order to keep my grade level up.

Daddy and a cousin in the Department of Education in Washington, DC, were busy trying to find me a new school, one that would appreciate my "unique characteristics." I realized now that I had caused Daddy a lot of trouble, something he did not need, especially now, and also a lot of money because they don't give refunds when you're expelled, as Mother so aptly pointed out. I knew I had a lot to make up for and I intended to study hard and make my peace with authority figures and rules.

Meeting a boy was the last thing on my mind, but it seems like those big moments in life come flying right out of the blue when you least expect them.

CHAPTER 52

Meeting Darryl

Age Sixteen

I met Darryl Jones when I was sixteen, on a Friday night at the Lion's Den in Vernon. It was a weekly sock hop sponsored by the city and located in a hall above the police station. After hearing all of the wild stories about him, that was the last place I would have expected to see him. When he arrived, I heard a hush come over the room and turned to see what everyone was looking at.

The sight of him took my breath away. He was leaning against the wall with one leg bent, his thumbs jammed into his jeans pocket, with a cigarette dangling from his lips. After much dithering among the chaperones, one of the little ladies walked up to him and said something. In response, he tipped his hat to her, walked to the door and flicked his cigarette outside. As he returned to his spot next to his buddy, I noticed he had the cockiest walk I had ever seen. Everyone was sneaking glances at him as they whispered to each other.

I had heard many stories about this boy from my friends and his granddaddy, Dick, but nothing had prepared me for the visceral response I was having to his mere presence. I was not alone; I could tell every other girl and probably half the women in the room would have sold their soul to be with him.

He looked like a tall drink of water to me, but he couldn't have been over five-feet-eleven, like most bronc and bull riders. He was wearing a white western shirt, tight jeans, and a fine pair of boots, sporting spurs that jangled when he walked. He had his head tilted down so he could discreetly survey the room while the brim of his black cowboy hat shielded his eyes. I could vaguely see black hair curling over his collar, olive skin, a perfect aquiline nose, and sensual, full lips.

I held my breath as I waited to see what he would do next, and I almost fainted as he started walking straight toward me. Stopping in front of me, he cleared his throat and said, "I'm Darryl Jones. Who are you?"

Trying to remain calm in spite of those piercing brown eyes staring right through me, I said, "I'm Rita Wharton." A look of recognition crossed his face for a fleeting second and then it was gone as quickly as it had come. He turned to look at all of the people watching us and a frown furrowed his brow. Even though he was only seventeen or eighteen, I could tell he felt old and out of place at this teenage shindig.

Watching him closely, I somehow knew this boy without any words being spoken, so I was not surprised when he turned back to me and said, "I have to get out of here. Do you want to go with me?"

I smiled and nodded, "Yes." Oblivious to all of the stares and whispers, I didn't care what anyone thought as he took my hand and led me out the door. The truth of the matter was, I would have followed him to hell and back.

His buddy drove us to the river and got out to have a smoke. Looking at me intently, he asked, "Have you heard anything about me?"

"Yes," I replied, "Diane is a good friend of mine."

Studying me for a minute, he asked, "So, how do you feel about that, about being with me, I mean?"

Breaking eye contact for the first time, he said, "And what about your Daddy?"

Laughing, I said, "Are you kidding? He and Dick are thicker than thieves. I think he'll be delighted."

Looking relieved, he was quiet for a moment and then a slow smile crossed his face as he said, "I've heard a lot of stories about you, too, but I won't hold them against you, either."

Bristling, I asked, "And what is that supposed to mean?"

Grinning now, he said, "Well, I heard you could out-ride and out-shoot almost every hombre in the county."

Looking at him intently, I asked, "And how do you feel about that?"

Looking just a little smug, he replied, "I'm not too worried about being beat by a girl. Especially a little girl like you."

Twisting my body around to get more leverage, I said, "Is that so?" I started tickling him with an expertise perfected over years of practicing on my brother. He bucked and squirmed, trying to get away from me, and finally yelled, "Calf rope! Calf rope! What I meant to say was, I can handle it."

One minute, we were laughing and wrestling like two playful puppies and the next, we were kissing in a way I had never been kissed. That soft, deep kiss awakened the fires of passion in me and I knew I had been waiting for this moment my whole life. Though I had just met him, I trusted him completely and did not hesitate to give myself to him. I knew he didn't think I was bad and Jesus knew what was in my heart, so I felt no shame. When he realized I was a virgin, he pulled back with a surprised look on his face. After searching my eyes for a long moment, he smiled and kissed me with the possessiveness of a boy that knows a girl belongs to him, body and soul. I had no idea what to expect, but I knew I wanted to be with him, become a part of him in any way I could.

After being with Darryl, I felt like a different person and I wondered if anyone would notice that I had become a woman. No one seemed to notice except Daddy, who was the last person I wanted to know about it. Being very discreet and respectful of my privacy, he never said a word, but I could tell he knew by the pensive look on his face when he looked at me now. I also knew he must have been steeling himself for this eventuality for quite some time because he was making a valiant effort to give Darryl a chance and even suggested that I invite him to dinner so they could get acquainted.

I had thought it would be just the family but at the last minute, guests arrived and Mother quickly upscaled to one of her highfalutin dinner parties. I could have kicked myself for not warning Darryl about all of the damned forks and spoons when I saw him eyeing them like they were rattlers lined up around his plate.

I was trying to catch his eye, but he was now focused on the lemon-scented finger cloth rolled up like a tight little bun. Horrified, I watched as he tentatively reached out, picked it up and put it into his mouth for an inquisitive bite. His surprise at finding the "bread" was a cloth registered on his face in ever-growing waves of embarrassment. My heart went out to him, but luckily, Daddy had also watched the scene unfold and immediately knew what to do. Reaching out for his cloth, he put it into his mouth and chomped down hard. Grimacing, he sputtered, "Dammit, Lu, what the hell are these things? I thought it was bread."

Looking absolutely nonplussed, my mother opened and closed her mouth, but not a word came out. Rarely at a loss for words, she quickly recovered and guided the conversation to safer ground.

Meanwhile, Darryl was looking very relieved and I was fighting back tears as I looked at Daddy with pure adoration and gratitude. He had saved my sweetheart in spite of his paternal instincts and I knew it was because the goodness in him would let him do no less.

The next evening, I snuggled up to Daddy and said, "So, what did you think?" He didn't have to ask what I was referring to, and answered, "Well, if he's anything like his granddaddy Dick, he can't be all bad. He seems to love you and he's not intimidated by you, so he might be a keeper."

I thought so too, but it made me feel a lot better hearing Daddy say so.

CHAPTER 53

The Newport School

Age Sixteen to Seventeen

My introduction to Newport, Rhode Island, began on a beautiful fall day as the leaves were turning brilliant shades of red and gold and the sea air was crisp and clean. We spent the first night at a quaint hotel near the ocean, and as I listened to the waves crashing into the steep cliffs, I felt as if I had been transported into the world of *Wuthering Heights*. My imagination ran wild and I felt alive in this place, invigorated by the natural, raw beauty and the bygone mysteries lurking in the dark walls of the magnificent, old mansions.

The Newport School for Girls was a European jewel transported to the point of the public Cliff Walk, high above the pounding surf. It was an exquisite small castle that had been moved, stone by stone, and I was thrilled to discover my room was in the round turret.

Newport was steeped in history and romance, but there was also electricity in the air. It seemed to have a faster heartbeat than Texas. My senses struggled out of the molasses pace I was accustomed to and quickened to this new, staccato beat. I was equally intrigued by the Yankee girls, even though they weren't overly friendly and seemed to derive a great deal of amusement from my accent and clothes.

I quickly realized that my matching pastel cashmere sweaters and skirts were terribly out of place here amid the madras and penny loafers. Even more critical, my coats were exceedingly inadequate to withstand the bone-chilling gales that blew off the ocean cliffs.

Thank God, I was finally accepted by "The Big Ten," a group of girls who, for all practical purposes, ran the school. Three of them were my roommates, but it was Robin who managed to get past my accent and wardrobe disasters long enough to get to know me. Up until then, I had merely been a Southern belle cliché to them and not worthy of their interest.

I gradually gained distinction because I was a Texan who actually lived on a ranch, tied my horse to the hitching post, shot real guns, and had oil wells in my backyard. I found them equally enthralling because they were intelligent and ambitious, with big career plans rather than expecting a debutante marriage of convenience. They didn't smile to your face and then stab you in the back. They just came right out and said what they meant and, even if it was hurtful, you always knew where you stood with them.

When they studied, they studied hard, but when they partied, they partied even harder. I had met my match in the arena of breaking rules as the poor headmistress, who teetered on the verge of a breakdown for two years, would testify. My most vivid memory was of her standing on a tabletop, screaming at the top of her lungs as she waved her fist in the air, "You call yourselves the Big Ten, don't think I don't know, but you are lower than a snake's belly!" Aside from the obvious slap-stick humor of the scene, I wondered how that little Yankee lady would know anything about a snake's belly.

As our class filed past the faculty to receive our diplomas at graduation, the last words the headmistress ever spoke to us elevated her to a new level of respect in our eyes. Handing us our diplomas, she smiled and hissed, "Good riddance."

I never realized how much I needed to confide in someone until I participated in the group therapy created by our close proximity and mutual trust. We all had our stories—different, but really just the same, and we found comfort in finally being able to tell them to people who would understand. Contrary to popular opinion, great wealth does not protect you from pain; it only adds to the scope and severity of the trials to be faced. Without judgment, we kept each other's secrets in sacred trust and supported one another's dreams.

We were also blessed with an incredible teaching staff. Our English teacher had a gift for making literature come alive and encouraged me to pursue my passion for writing. Our math teacher, somehow, made me understand geometry, despite my left-brain handicap. And our political science teacher forced us to think for ourselves and accept our responsibility as voting members of a democratic society. She made sure we kept up with current events by requiring us to write a paragraph on each article from *Newsweek* and *Time* magazines.

Little did we know that in April of 1963, we would read about the heartbreak of her life. Her husband was in the Navy on a nuclear submarine, the USS *Thrasher*, when it imploded in deep waters off the coast of Cape Cod. It was the first US nuclear submarine to be lost at sea, and it took all lives aboard. The tragedy was astonishing to the American people, but it was even more horrific for us because we saw the devastating loss on the anguished face of our beloved teacher.

Consequently, we were glad we had the Kennedys to focus on. They exuded energy and boisterous fun when they were in town and we were always hopeful we would catch a glimpse of the president. The Secret Service were accustomed to the Newport girls' daily trek from the old mansion that served as the senior dorm to the main building and would smile indulgently when the Kennedy children yelled and waved to us. They seemed like a golden family, happy and healthy, giving us all hope and faith in the future.

CHAPTER 54

Home for Christmas

Age Seventeen

When I arrived home for Christmas, I immediately sensed something wasn't right. The house was decorated, as usual, but there was a sad silence I couldn't put my finger on. As I went in search of Daddy, I suddenly realized what was missing: It was Daddy's boyish exuberance that always filled the house at Christmas time. We all lived Christmas through him because he still had a childlike belief in magic that most people only get to keep for a short while. When he said he believed in Santa Claus, you believed him because he made it so. He touched the child in us and filled us with happy expectation.

Today, there was only silence. There was no usual greeting at the front door as he bellowed, "Merry Christmas! Merry Christmas!" while madly shaking the sleigh bells around his neck and looking stupid in his Santa Claus hat and red plaid shirt.

I found Mother sitting at her desk in the office, simply staring into space. When I entered the room, she tried to rally for my greeting, but her smile was wooden and her eyes looked dead.

Alarmed by her demeanor, I asked, "What's wrong? Where's Daddy?" Her eyes watering slightly, she said, "He's upstairs in his dressing room."

We all knew that was Daddy's cave when he was troubled, so I hesitated as I asked, "Can I go up?"

Smiling wanly, Mother said, "Of course. You'll cheer him up."

As I started up the stairs, Mother said, "Rita, wait. I don't know if this is the right thing to do, but I feel you should know what's happened so you can help your father as much as possible. Our attorneys have just informed us that someone has juggled the books to show Buster owes the Waggoner Estate three million instead of them owing him. He's devastated. Not just because of the money, but because he can't believe his own family would do this to him. They're trying to squeeze him out, so they're taking advantage of the fact that he's so gravely ill. They know what this is costing him physically, but they can't even let him die in peace."

Seeing the look of horror on my face, she exclaimed, "I'm sorry. I know you haven't accepted that yet. Go on up to your father. Oh, Rita, one more thing, as the attorneys were going over the books, they discovered one of your father's most trusted employees has been embezzling money from him. He won't tell me who it is, but he's terribly hurt."

As I walked into the darkened room, I saw Daddy sitting on the couch, silently staring out the window. Quietly sitting next to him, I kissed him and said, "Hi, Daddy. I'm home."

He looked like someone waking from the dead as he struggled to come out of his lethargy to greet me. Trying to focus, he put his hands on my shoulders and stared at me hard. Finally, he said, "You look good. That Yankee school must agree with you."

Smiling, I replied, "It does, Daddy. Who would have thought? Thank you for finding it for me. I won't let you down this time. I think I've found my place."

Looking somewhat distracted, he said, "Good. Good. I'm glad to hear that."

As my eyes grew accustomed to the dark, I saw how frail he looked and I couldn't believe how much he had changed just since August. Taking his hand, I said, "Mother told me about all the trouble."

Patting my hand, he said, "Oh, I wish she hadn't bothered you with that."

Stroking those beloved few hairs left on the top of his head, I said, "It's no bother. Is there anything I can do, Daddy?"

Looking up at me and then back down, he said, "No, honey. I don't expect there's anything anyone can do. Except, maybe, the lawyers. That's the best we can hope for, I'm afraid. What a damn fool I've been. I probably deserve this, but you don't. That's what sticks in my craw."

Straining to see his eyes in the dim light, I said, "I want you to stop worrying about me, Daddy. I'll be fine, no matter what happens. You made me a survivor. Besides, I've got a sidekick that will take care of me. You know that."

Looking bemused, he said, "Yes, I do. And I've never been as glad about that as I am right now."

Seeing the sadness return to his face, I asked, "Are you sad about your family, Daddy?

Quiet for a moment, he said, "You're my family now—you, your mother, Bucky, Pa, and Mommy Bobbie. I have no other family, they've made that perfectly clear."

After a brief silence, I asked "Are you upset about the man who cheated you?"

Sighing deeply, Daddy replied, "I'm just sorry he didn't feel he could come to me and tell me he needed more money. I would have given it to him. But then, it seems I'm not a very good judge of character, either." I didn't know what to say to that, so we sat quietly in the dark, holding on to what little time we had left.

The next day, Shorty Switzer came to take Daddy hunting. While Big Charles helped him get ready, I went to say hello to Shorty and with the niceties dispensed with, I asked him, point blank, "Do you think he's up to hunting? He looks awfully weak to me."

Quick to get my drift, he said, "Oh, don't you worry. We don't do much shootin'. We just find us a shady spot and chew the fat for a while. He just likes being outside, it makes him feel better."

Giving him a quick hug, I said, "You're so right, Shorty. Thanks for being such a good friend."

Just then, Big Charles came walking towards us, holding Daddy in his arms. As Shorty and Big Charles exchanged a protective, knowing look, Daddy was gently transferred into Shorty's arms.

I watched in grateful silence as that short, pot-bellied little man performed his labor of love and carried Daddy to the hunting wagon. A welder, he had run the Headquarters Shop of the ranch; he had ridden and hunted by Daddy's side, and now they would finish it together. As I watched the two of them, I suddenly knew I was right—my father was a well-loved man and an excellent judge of character.

CHAPTER 55

Daddy Dies

Age Seventeen

Even though I liked my new school, leaving Daddy was the hardest thing I had ever done. I had seen how fast Charles took a turn for the worse, and Newport was so far away. But at least I knew I was leaving him in good hands because Mother watched over him like a hawk, monitoring all of his food and medicine with an eagle eye.

Because Daddy had always rallied before, she let herself believe that she could keep him alive with constant, perfect care. Daddy encouraged her denial and suggested Hawaii might be just what he needed to perk him up. Since he did not have the strength to fight the lawsuit, Mother was handling it for him with a deadly resolve. She rarely smiled or laughed anymore, and I knew he was worried about her. Perhaps he knew the end was near and simply wanted their last months together to be filled with the perfume of gardenias and the lush beauty of the islands.

Whatever the reason for their sad insanity, she packed them up and hauled her dying husband to his magical island. Out of their shared love of beauty and fantasy, they created a world where miracles were possible and they could believe he really would get well.

Sadly, that was not the case, and Mother had to transport him, in critical condition, to Baylor Hospital in Dallas. Never leaving his side, she tended to him night and day, even cooking his meals on a rotisserie they had sent from the ranch. Daddy didn't have much of an appetite anymore and she hoped to entice him with her orange, honey-glazed duck and Cornish hens. But in spite of her efforts, food belonged to the land of the living and he quietly slipped into a coma.

I was not surprised when I received the dreaded call, but I was shocked that Mother had waited so long to call me. I had practiced this moment a thousand times in my head, but I had never pictured Daddy in a coma and I felt cheated. Charles and I had gotten to say our goodbyes, and I was devastated to think Daddy and I would never speak again. There was so much I wanted to tell him, so when I got to the hospital, I immediately pulled a chair up by his bed, took his hand in both of mine, and laying my cheek on it, I began to whisper my last words of love and farewell. And I prayed. I prayed for a miracle. I prayed for his sweet release if a miracle wasn't in the cards. His organs were shutting down one by one and his every breath was a struggle. The doctors said nothing more could be done and that they had no idea what was keeping him alive.

Bucky had arrived shortly after me and we watched in anguish as Daddy fought for every breath of air. Poor Pa, Daddy's father, could no longer bear to watch and sat with his head on his wife's shoulder, crying softly. Mama and Avis watched in helpless silence as Mother, looking like a disheveled, waxen figure, stared at his labor in resigned disbelief, knowing there was nothing she could do now. That may have been the only time in her life that she didn't care about how she looked.

In answer to our prayers, a dear friend, Dr. Peggy Dyer, arrived to check on us. She was not one of his doctors but was working under Dr. Mills, a brilliant plastic surgeon. Seeing our distress, she said, "His breathing is so labored because his lungs are filling up with blood. I can't make him any better, but I can make him more comfortable by removing the blood. Would you like me to do that?" We all breathed at once, "Yes, please."

I don't think I had ever felt more grateful in my whole life. Peggy had been on duty for twenty-four hours straight, but she stayed the rest of the night, sucking the blood out of his lungs with a small rubber tube. He seemed to rest easy, at last, and I had almost dozed off, holding onto his hand, when he suddenly said, "Deets, what day is it?"

Stunned, I exclaimed, "Daddy, you're awake!"

In a more urgent tone, Daddy asked, "What's the date?"

Thinking for a moment, I said, "It's May 28th, Daddy. Why?"

With a soft sigh, he whispered, "Good. I made it. You'll be okay now." Then, he closed his eyes and seemed to drift off into a peaceful sleep, never to wake again.

He died within the hour as we looked on in grief-stricken disbelief. I suddenly realized Bucky was no longer in the room and I went to look for him. I found him in the hall, staring out at the rain falling in the gray light of dawn. After a few moments of silently watching the rain together, I finally said, "Mama says when it rains, it's God crying for the loss we feel when someone dies. I like that idea."

Still staring out the window, Bucky said, "Now we'll never get to know each other better."

Turning to face him, I said, "Daddy loved you. That's all that matters."

Looking at his face, gray in this somber light, I realized he was in a terrible place, far worse than the rest of us. If we were in hell, he was in purgatory, not knowing what he should feel about that dead man in there who had called him son. I could tell he felt numb and alone, with only guilt and regret for company. My heart broke for him as I watched him struggle to find some sense of belonging, some sense of real loss for his father's death. How could he ever reconcile what he had been told and what he had experienced with Daddy? Seeing his pain, I thought it was a tragic waste and the cruelest of life's jokes.

After we returned to the hotel, Mother suggested we order some food, even though no one was very hungry. When I heard a knock on the door, I opened it, thinking it was room service. A strange man in a suit, holding a large manila envelope, stood in front of me and asked, "May I speak to your mother?"

I called Mother and stood listening as the man said, "I'm here to tell you that the trial that was supposed to be concluded today has been postponed. You will find the new trial date in these papers. Please let us know if that date meets with your approval. We are terribly sorry for your loss."

I suddenly realized the impact of what he was saying and I felt a rage that threatened to consume me. That was why Daddy had hung on so long, why he had suffered so much. That was why he had asked what day it was. For the first time in my life, I wanted to physically hurt someone and I lunged at the man, screaming, "How dare you come here? My father just died. Are you happy now? Isn't that what you wanted? You're all a bunch of heartless vultures." Mother and Pa pulled me off of the man and Pa led me to the bedroom, where I collapsed in inconsolable sobs. That day, instead of food, I received an injection from the hotel doctor so I could go to sleep and hide in sweet oblivion.

CHAPTER 56

Daddy's Wake

Age Seventeen

Even though Daddy was supposed to be buried in the family plot in Fort Worth—only a few feet away from Charles, oddly enough—we took him home to the land and people he loved. Everything was done according to the old ways, and he lay in state at our house for three days so his friends could pay their respects.

It seemed there was an endless stream of people circulating through the house, some crying softly and others telling their favorite stories about Buster. Mother and I greeted them all and thanked them for their kind support, especially those who had come from other states and countries.

I could feel nothing. It was like I had died inside, but my body continued to function in a rote manner. I glanced over at Daddy from time to time, thinking how strange it was that his appearance had improved with death. He looked pink cheeked and healthy, with all signs of the jaundice gone. I had grown so used to the faint, yellowish tinge to his skin that I had forgotten how rosy and young he could look. That was what he should have looked like, if it hadn't been for the liquor. My enemy had won this battle, but I was going to make sure it didn't have the last say. He lived with pain so long that he had developed a habit of grinding or locking his teeth when he wasn't speaking. Now, his faint smile was relaxed and soft like a baby's and I was grateful that he was free at last.

I made a mental note to write the funeral home a letter of special thanks for their kind and painstaking service. Suddenly, I saw a figure coming toward me and even though the light from behind made him a silhouette, I would have known that walk anywhere. Not caring what anyone thought,

I flew into his arms and held on tight. I felt a flicker of life in me and I was glad to know that I could still feel something. Pa came up from behind me, introduced himself to Darryl and suggested he take me outside for a break.

Ever so grateful, I kissed Pa and snuggled against Darryl as we walked to my favorite secret place by the pond. Once we were settled on the bench, Darryl's eyes scanned the horizon as he asked, "Do you want to talk about it?"

Looking back at me, he waited until I was ready and once I started speaking, I didn't stop until I had told him everything. Holding me, he listened intently until I was done, and then said softly, "I'm sorry." It was enough because of the way he said it. I knew he understood and shared my pain. I loved the fact that he had dropped everything and came to me the minute he heard the news. It wasn't always easy loving a cowboy, with their rolling stone ways, but our souls were in tune and he always gave me what I needed, including my freedom.

When we returned to the house, Rosie told me that Mother and our attorney, Elton Hyder, wanted to see us up in the playroom, away from our guests. When Darryl gave me a questioning look, I shrugged my shoulders and said, "You got me."

Once introductions were out of the way, Elton leaned back and stared at Darryl before he said, "Lu tells me Rita plans to marry you."

Horrified, I thought I might die of embarrassment as Darryl turned a slow smile my way. Before I could deny the charge, Darryl took my hand and in a steady voice, said, "Yes, sir. Someday, I want us to get married and have a ranch of our own, but right now, I've got other plans. Rita understands that."

Looking somewhat amused, Elton asked, "And do you mind telling me what those plans are?"

Warming to his subject, Darryl grinned and said, "Of course not, sir. I'm going on the rodeo circuit. I plan on being world champion."

Whatever Elton had expected to hear, it certainly wasn't that, and the blank look on his face was testimony to his complete bewilderment. I was enjoying this immensely because I had never seen Elton Hyder at a loss for words. I could tell this wasn't going anything like he had expected.

Finally, regaining his composure, he chuckled and said, "Dear boy, surely you understand that Rita will run this ranch and will need a strong man by her side who is willing to help her do just that. I understand you grew up on a ranch, too, and that is good, but you must also be able to help her with critical business decisions, as well. Now, my suggestion is this. We will be happy to pay for your college education as well as your law degree, in order to prepare you for your future role." Feeling very magnanimous, Elton leaned back, once again, and asked, "So what do you think of that idea?"

Once Darryl had recovered from his shock, he held up his hands and shook his head, saying, "Whoa, sir. That's a very generous offer, but that's not me. Cowboying is the only thing I ever want to do, it's what I'm good at." Smiling self-consciously, he continued, "Besides, why should I do something against my nature when Rita's got a fine attorney like you? I'm sure she could hire a lot of good attorneys, but I'd like to think there's not a lot of men that could be her partner. But I sure do appreciate the offer, sir. It was mighty kind of you."

Elton sat staring at Darryl, totally perplexed, as he remembered sleeping on aluminum counters where he washed dishes while working his way through law school. He recognized someone else's passion, even though it was so different from his own. Just past the bewilderment, I could see respect in Elton's eyes as he leaned over to shake Darryl's hand, saying, "Well, thanks for hearing me out, son. Best of luck to you."

Darryl, taking his cue, said, "Thank you, sir. Mrs. Wharton, my sincere condolences." Looking at me, he mouthed, "I'll see you downstairs."

Once he left, I proudly waited to hear Elton's opinion of Darryl. I knew he was his own person, for better or worse, and could not be bought. Elton Hyder was a force to be reckoned with, as any attorney who had gotten their tail feathers singed by him in a courtroom would tell you. At eighteen, Darryl had stood up to him and held his own. I was proud, as any country girl would be, to have such a man. Raised to look for the best in every breed, the survivors, a country girl knew a boy with survival skills when she saw one.

Unfortunately, we don't always live up to our potential, especially after life chews us up and spits us out. But for the moment, I was content to bask in the look of approval on Elton's face as he said, "Exceptional young man. Reminds me of myself at his age. Pretty independent, isn't he? But then, he better be if he's gonna be your man. Now, go on down and get that boy some food."

As I left the room, I kissed Elton, whispering, "Thank you," and then kissing Mother, I said, "Thank you, Mother. It was a sweet thought."

I knew Darryl had to follow his dream in order to outrun his past, so I supported him in his goal. I also knew he would run at the end of summer, but I was grateful he was making time for me now. He took me with him to several nearby rodeos and I learned to smile that wooden smile that all rodeo wives and girlfriends wear after they have just watched the man they love get stomped into the ground. I had been around rodeos and cowboys all of my life, but it looked a whole lot different when it was my love catapulting off the horns of a bull. After one very close call, tears stung my eyes as he limped towards me and put his arms around me. I never made a sound, but after a minute, he lifted my chin so he could see my face and said, softly, "You know you can't come if it's going to upset you like this. I have to focus and I can't be worried about you. I'm gonna take a lot of falls, that's just the way it is. Can you handle it?"

Taking a deep breath, I smiled my biggest smile and said, "I can handle it." I did handle it, but only because I got so good at wearing a brave mask. Darryl was the only other person I knew who liked to ride at night so we also had our quiet, alone time. We could ride for hours in companionable silence, soothed by the rhythmic movements of our horses and the feel of cool evening breezes playing across our skin as we listened to the coyotes singing in the distance. Sometimes, we would speculate on the vastness of the universe and lament the fact that we had been born too late, at least a hundred years too late. We were like young dinosaurs witnessing our own extinction, and even though we knew it was coming, there wasn't a damn thing we could do about it.

So we did the only thing we could do. We tried to make the most of what little time we had left and somehow imprint an indelible picture on our minds so we would never forget that we had walked this land. One of our favorite places, Medicine Mounds, was near his stepfather's ranch and had been so named for the three large mounds inexplicably rising out of the flat, red dirt landscape. Quanah Parker, the Great Chief of the Comanches, considered them sacred ground and used them for vision quests and tribal ceremonies. The area was a treasure trove of fossils and other artifacts, but we never took anything out of reverence for the sacred spirits there.

We also spent a lot of time at his stepfather's ranch so Darryl could help out with the horses when he was home. The crown jewel of the ranch was the huge, circular horse barn and arena that housed the champion quarter horses that Oscar Dodsen was known for. He ran a lucrative stud service and since Avis had bred several of her mares to his stallions, I had been there many times before. But now, if Darryl was working, I went to the house to visit with his mother, Leatrice.

The first time I saw her, I knew where Darryl had gotten his stunning good looks. She was one of the most beautiful women I had ever seen, but in a natural way, unlike a lot of the wealthy, well-maintained women who came to our house. Daddy called those women "high-maintenance," and said he never wanted me to be like them. Since I was a girl who lived in jeans, I told Daddy he was preaching to the choir.

I loved being with Leatrice and her two little twin girls and baby boy who could melt your heart with one slurpy wet kiss. It's amazing how babies can perk a girl right up, and I was grateful for the reprieve from perpetual sadness. She, in turn, welcomed me warmly because I loved her son. And as I watched her chase the kids around, I envisioned Darryl and me with our children on a ranch of our own. I figured five little cowpokes would make a good crew for him to ride herd over. Sadly, that was not meant to be, but we maintained a lifelong friendship that I cherished. He would go on to become "Mr. Winston" in cigarette commercials, and his image was plastered on billboards across the country. Even though he never became the world champion bronc rider he set out to be, he was inducted into the Cowboy Hall of Fame years later for his contributions to rodeo and the cowboy way of life.

CHAPTER 57

Life Without Daddy

Age Seventeen

For some unknown reason, LaRita insisted on Bucky's return to Albuquerque immediately after the funeral. Mother begged her to let him stay because Pa and Mommy Bobbie were going to be with us for a couple of weeks and Mother thought it would be good for all of us to be together. Nevertheless, LaRita remained adamant and it wouldn't be long before we knew why.

Meanwhile, I was trying to adjust to the ranch and our home without Daddy. An empty sadness filled the house, particularly when Sissy, my mother's oldest toy poodle, sat at the foot of the stairs and howled for hours at a time. Years ago, she had adopted Daddy and overcome his aversion to small, yapping dogs. No longer able to snuggle up on his lap, she cried for all of us as we struggled back to the land of the living. The servants were convinced that Daddy's spirit remained in his dressing room, and Rosie, who refused to go up there, said, "I sure 'nough did love Mr. Buster, but I don't want no business with no ghostie. No siree."

I prayed they were right, and it seemed I, too, could feel his presence—wishful thinking, perhaps, but it gave me comfort. I spent a lot of time in his room looking at his little treasures and breathing in the smell of him that still lingered there. I sat on the couch gazing at his heavy, carved oak desk, his workout corner, and his shop area where he made little model cars and branded anything that could fit in the house. How he loved to putter with his hands, like the detailed map of the ranch he created with colored pencils, which was later printed and made into post cards for the ranch. His love of life and his sense of humor echoed throughout the room and sweet memories flooded over me as I looked at the ceramic pheasant with its miniature straw hat, cocked at a jaunty angle. Any time he passed it, he made sure the hat was still in place, saying, "Looking good, señor."

Daddy found childlike delight in attending to funny little details such as that and the multitude of clocks he wound and maintained throughout the house. He truly enjoyed all of his possessions, from the least to the greatest, and loved to share his bounty with his family and friends. He made his barber a millionaire and helped several men in Vernon start their own businesses. They were his hunting buddies; that's just what you did for friends. To him it was very simple—he had money and they didn't. With the exception of a handful of close friends, it was those men who still came to visit him on a regular basis, even though he could no longer take them hunting, throw a fun party, or loan them money. He treasured their friendship and was always in better spirits by the time they left.

Now, as I looked around the room, I saw all of the photos he had taken over the years—images of the people and places he loved most. Wealthy, famous people were placed side by side with ordinary friends; their frames touched each other, along with beloved employees and pets. I smiled as I thought about the rich life he had lived and the many hearts he had touched, and I was grateful he had left me so many golden memories to fill the huge space he left behind. It was as if some life spark in the land had died with Daddy, and there was no place on the ranch that I could escape the awful emptiness. After drifting aimlessly and alone for days, I finally sought comfort with Pa, who was suffering as much as I was. He was the only thing I had left of Daddy and I wanted to make the most of every minute with him.

Mother walked through her duties like some lifeless doll, not seeking comfort from anyone. She was consumed with guilt and remorse and did not seem to feel she deserved any comfort. The magnitude of her loss was beginning to sink in, so she dared not let her guard down for an instant. She knew a nasty battle lay ahead and she wasn't sure she was up to it without her champion; so, she drank—not during the day, and only after her work was done, but she drank. Her old friend, Smirnoff, was there every night to bolster her courage and kill her pain. Her drinking widened the gulf between us, so we found no comfort in one another. I had hoped our mutual loss would make us closer, but that was not to be. Our polite civility was turning into sullen anger, so I sought refuge with my friends, which was the beginning of a lifelong pattern.

Jim Greenwood was my creative friend who introduced me to Larry McMurtry, no doubt hoping the author would light a literary fire under me. Disgusted by my infatuation with men, he would snort, "You're like a beautiful bird in a golden cage. You'll never be a writer if you don't stop kowtowing to boys." Unlike me, Jim did follow his heart; he became an editor for the newspaper in Aspen, Colorado.

Mike Hardage was my hunting buddy and fellow Christian. Though I rarely shared my religious beliefs with anyone, we were comfortable discussing all of the taboo topics: religion, sex, politics, and psychology. He could sing like an angel, much like his cousin, Roy Orbison, and though I enjoyed hearing him sing in church, I loved it when he played guitar and sang Johnny Cash's "Long Black Veil" and "Tennessee Stud." We were two odd ducks who recognized each other immediately and supported one another in our right to be different.

John Christopher, on the other hand, was my all-American friend who had transferred to Vernon from California. His father was in the service so he was accustomed to moving a lot, which made him an extremely adaptable people-person. He never met a stranger and was that rare guy that everyone liked. He was also the best all-around athlete I had ever known, and his backhand on the tennis court was lethal. All of these golden qualities made his accident even more tragic. Ever the nice guy, he got into the car with a fifteen-year-old boy who had just gotten his driver's permit and needed someone to accompany him. They had a head-on collision with a car being driven by a pregnant woman, killing her and the baby. John was catapulted into the air and scraped along the pavement for at least a hundred feet. When Gary called to tell me what had happened, he said the prognosis was not good, and that it would probably be better if he died. The doctors and nurses obviously didn't know who they were dealing with, and after numerous surgeries and endless setbacks, John went on to college and got married. He taught me the true meaning of courage as I watched him come back, time after time, never quitting.

Darryl and I spent most of our time hanging out with his two best friends, Bob Ferguson and Horace Joe Tabor, who would become my lifelong friends and two of the nicest men I've ever known. Bob was the true blue, level-headed friend you could always count on. We almost lost him to another horrific car accident that crushed his face, necessitating the invention of a new head apparatus and the rebuilding of his face from a photo. Since his lips were numb after so many surgeries, we practiced his kissing before he started dating again, much to everyone's great amusement. The doctor did a fabulous job, and Bob's good looks were not lost, as his future wife, Lana, would testify.

Horace Joe loved to party, but he knew where to draw the line, and I knew I could count on him to keep Darryl safe. If anyone had told me he would end up being my banker, I would not have believed it, but he did, much to my good fortune. Darryl knew how much I enjoyed having Bob and Horace Joe with us, so I was shocked one night when he told them we needed to be alone.

Conditioned to expect the worst, I immediately asked, "What's wrong? What's happened?"

Trying to allay my fears, he quickly said, "Nothing. Nothing. We just need to talk."

"About what?" I asked as the fear began to rise inside and threatened to choke me.

Clearing his throat, he said, "Well, you know the rodeo is coming up."

Growing more frustrated by the minute, I said, "Yes. I know."

Looking miserable, he mumbled, "Well, I was wondering if you'd want to ride with me in the grand entry?"

Thoroughly relieved, I squealed, "Yes. I'd love to."

Still looking cautious, he said, "Rita, you know it will brand you as mine, don't you? Are you sure you want to do that?"

Smiling at him softly, I said, "I'm positive. Can we wear matching shirts?"

Looking somewhat dubious, he said, "You bet, as long as they're not covered in pink roses or some damn thing."

The night of the rodeo, we rode like the wind, wild and free, wearing our blue-and-purple western shirts. We belonged together and we didn't care if the whole world knew it.

CHAPTER 58

The Hearing

Age Seventeen

It was only a few weeks before our attorneys informed us that LaRita had joined forces with the Waggoner Estate in order to take our part of the ranch. Stunned, I suddenly knew why she had insisted on Bucky's return to Albuquerque immediately after the funeral. In order to protect the ranch from fortune hunters, the estate had been set up to give control to every other generation, with only the children, rather than husbands or wives, able to inherit. Consequently, Electra Waggoner's will, rather than Daddy's, would determine our fate. Knowing this, Daddy had tried to protect me by stating in his will that anyone trying to take my inheritance would automatically forfeit any personal property they would have otherwise inherited. Unfortunately, my attorneys did not think it would be an effective deterrent because there was so much more at stake. We were talking about at least $75,000,000 in liquid assets and approximately 250,000 acres, so Daddy's jewelry, gun collection, oil royalties, and small amount of property in Fort Worth were a drop in the bucket by comparison.

Seeing how hurt I was, Elton Hyder rushed to reassure me regarding Bucky, saying, "Now, Rita, don't take this personal; it's not Bucky doing this. He's only fifteen, and it's his mother's call as his guardian. Since you and Bucky are both underage, your mothers will run the show. Besides, Buster knew LaRita had this planned from the day Bucky was born; he just didn't know exactly how it would all shake out. I know Buster warned you about this, so you're going to have to get over any hurt feelings you may have. This is war, and sentiment won't win the day. Now, the thing we have going for us is the fact that Electra's will refers to any beneficiary's children as 'lawful issue' rather than the customary 'matrimonial issue'. She suspected both of her sons were sterile, and she deliberately used the term, 'lawful', because she didn't think either of them could have natural children. And since you are adopted, that legal wording is very good for us because it implies that she knew any grandchildren would have to be adopted."

I sat in shocked silence as I realized the far-reaching implications of this information. Thinking back to when Mother and Daddy had tried to have a baby, I asked, "Why did Electra think Daddy was sterile?"

Looking a bit uncomfortable, Elton replied, "One of his testicles never came down. She had been told he couldn't have children." I remembered when Mother and Daddy had gone to see a specialist in Switzerland, hoping he could give them the answer they wanted to hear. Unfortunately, they returned with dashed hopes, but I never knew why. They just told me I would not be getting a new brother or sister, after all.

Elton was addressing me again, saying, "The Waggoner Estate is helping Bucky because they think he will sell out as soon as they eliminate you. You are a threat because you grew up on the ranch and love it, whereas Bucky and his mother have never cared much about the ranch. It's just that simple. They will use him to get rid of you."

Thinking back on all of the things Daddy had warned me about, I was amazed by the accuracy of his sad predictions.

The first hearing was scheduled for June and I was looking forward to seeing Bucky. When he stepped off the elevator at the courthouse, I ran to greet him, but his attorneys blocked my path. Hurt and confused, I allowed my attorney, George Kemble, to lead me into the courtroom as he whispered, "They don't want you talking to him. They will only tell him what they want him to know."

As the hearing got underway, I was surprised to hear them call Daddy's uncle, E. Paul Waggoner, to the witness stand. After answering several general questions regarding the family, E. Paul caused an explosion of shocked gasps as he stated in a very matter-of-fact manner that it was common knowledge in the family that both Buster and his brother, Tom, were sterile—Tom due to syphilis he had contracted as a teenager, and Buster due to an undescended testicle.

As my mouth fell open like everyone else's, I thought Daddy's uncle must be having a senior moment or a mental breakdown. Quickly looking over at Bucky's attorneys, I was surprised to see their calm demeanor. Beyond them, I saw Bucky, his face white as a sheet, staring ahead in wide-eyed confusion as he tried to understand what this meant for him.

I whispered to my attorney, "I don't understand what's going on. Can we have a recess?"

Once in private chambers, Elton Hyder said, "That was pretty crafty, I'll give 'em that.

They're going for a win-win situation here. If we play the illegitimate card they've offered us, we can probably eliminate Bucky, but it could come back to bite us in the butt!"

Interrupting him, I said, "I already told you I won't do that. As far as I'm concerned, Bucky is Daddy's son, no matter what E. Paul or the doctors say. Besides, you said it wouldn't guarantee my winning, and I won't hurt Bucky like that."

Elton, looking over at George Kemble, smiled slyly as he said, "Pretty smooth move on their part. Throwing that bone out there could have pitted Rita against Bucky, thus setting up the possibility that they would eliminate each other, saving the Waggoner Estate a lot of time and money. I'll bet you ten-to-one that's what they were hoping for, but we can use it against them. They don't know Rita wouldn't consider that. We'll let 'em sweat it out!"

Speaking up again, I said, "I would rather see Bucky win than allow the Biggses to take it all. I mean it."

Patting my hand reassuringly, George said, "Don't worry, Honey. I don't think it will come to that. There are a lot of powerful men in this country with adopted children who don't want to see a negative legal precedent established in the courts."

George Kemble, my personal attorney, was an old-school, Southern gentleman who treated me like a daughter and always brought me gardenias from his garden. He had very bad emphysema and had to sleep sitting up some nights. I knew what a dreadful toll this case was taking on him, but I was grateful for his kindness and understanding. Now, as I listened to his reassuring words, I hoped he was right, but something told me we were in for a rough ride.

When Electra Waggoner's will was executed in the 1920s, the adoption law in existence did not have the later language, added during the 1950s, that broadened the term *issue* to include adopted children, unless specifically negated in the will. Therefore, they could argue that Electra did not have adopted children in mind when she used the terms *lawful issue* and *the persons next eventually entitled under the terms of my will,* and because I was adopted, it was ruled that I could not be a legitimate heir.

After what seemed like hours of legal mumbo jumbo, I suddenly sat up and took notice when the judge said that Mother and I had one year to vacate the ranch, until such time as the case was resolved. My head began to spin and I thought I might be sick. First Daddy, and now, my home. I couldn't imagine my life without the ranch and I had no idea where we would go.

When the hearing concluded, I was determined to talk to Bucky, so as we left the courtroom, I hurried over to him and grabbed his hand, pulling him after me. When his attorneys tried to retrieve him, Elton interceded and distracted them with a lot of legalese. As they cast nervous glances our way, I talked fast, saying, "Don't believe everything you hear in there. They'll say anything to win. You're still my brother and I love you. Even if they take everything else, they can never take that away. Remember that. We'll get through this."

Waving sadly to each other, we parted not knowing it would be years before we saw each other again.

CHAPTER 59

Revolution and Death

Age Seventeen to Eighteen

I returned to school with a heavy heart. I missed Daddy and I dreaded the thought of leaving the ranch. I was also worried about Darryl and not just because he could get seriously hurt or killed. There was a reason why they wrote country and western songs about *that damned ol' rodeo*. She could steal your man and never give him back, bouncing him from one rodeo to the next until he was a beat-up, worn-out pile of broken bones. Rodeo was a banshee siren that dangled that gold buckle until a cowboy was left bitter and broken in the end. I didn't want that to happen to Darryl, neither to his body nor his soul, but I knew better women than me had gone a round with Rodeo and lost. You could fill every honky-tonk in Texas with the river of tears cried by the women who had lost their men to rodeo. I did not intend to be one of them, but I knew I was in for a rough time. Plus, there were all kinds of two-stepping fillies that would love to lasso Darryl and I wouldn't be there to stop them.

I knew I must not let myself dwell on things I couldn't change, so I recalled the words of two of the smartest women I knew. Grace always said, "Rid your mind of negative thoughts," and Mama said, "Have faith and expect the best," so that's just what I tried to do.

Newport was an intriguing, beautiful place, but New York and Boston set me on fire. The galleries, the theaters, the restaurants, and the hustle-bustle tempo of those magnificent cities conquered my aversion to urban areas and would forever draw me back. Though I could never live in a city, they energized me in a marvelous way when taken in small doses.

Everything seemed more intense on the East Coast and you could almost feel a palpable, revolutionary undercurrent seething below the pavement. The Civil Rights Movement and the Vietnam War were polarizing people into warring factions, ripping families apart and dividing the country at the Mason-Dixon Line.

The first time I got arrested for marching for civil rights and for protesting the Vietnam War, my mother said she was glad my father was not alive to witness my disgrace. I rather thought Daddy would have marched with me, in spite of being friends with Eisenhower and calling himself a Republican. My farming and ranching friends at home were saying it was their patriotic duty to defend democracy and fight communism in Vietnam, just as the poor and expendable have always been encouraged to believe. These were boys I had grown up with and the thought of them dying in some mosquito-infested swamp, in a country that did not want us or our democracy, was more than I could bear; and for what? Nothing except fear, as far as I could tell, so I took an unpopular stand against the war, little knowing I had just taken my first step toward joining the ranks of American youth in the bitter struggle between the generations.

Make love, not war! would one day be our battle cry, but for the moment, we were a nation living the American dream, with a young, vibrant president who embodied all that America stood for. His heartfelt challenge, "Ask not what your country can do for you, but what you can do for your country," lit a fire of optimism that promised to make us invincible—or so we thought, until that fateful day in Dallas that changed everything and ended the Camelot years. Forever after, people would ask that wrenching question, "Where were you the day John F. Kennedy was killed?"

I could hardly have been in a worse place on that tragic day because I was a Texan on a train bound for New York. I was going to see a friend who had graduated from Newport the year before and was now attending college in the city. I first heard the news in Princeton, where they had just canceled their big game out of respect for the president. A young man who had boarded the train there quietly told us of the president's death and discreetly suggested that I not speak because of my Texas accent. Grief-stricken and not knowing who to blame, most people chose to hate Texas for letting him die there. I couldn't argue with that, so I suffered another major loss, alone in my grief, surrounded by people who would hate me if I tried to share my pain. JFK had been my hero as well as the hope of a nation, and I wondered how any of us would survive such a loss.

My friend's brother met me at Grand Central and spoke not a word as we walked through the almost dead, silent train station. The only sound to be heard was the crying of grieving people huddled in groups, comforting one another, and the occasional solitary soul who stood alone, staring into space, shock chiseled on their face.

Once in the car, we saw long panels of black cloth hanging from the windows of hotel rooms Jack Kennedy had frequented. New York was in mourning and seemed to hush her noisy babel out of respect for her dead president, almost as if the heartbeat of a nation had stopped when Kennedy died.

My friend's brother finally spoke before he let me out in front of his sister's dorm, saying, "I'm sorry. I know it's irrational, but I can't get past the fact that you're a Texan. I hope we'll meet again under better circumstances." I nodded in agreement and turned to enter the building, hoping with all my heart that his sister, Mary Jane, didn't feel the same way. Luckily, she did not and quickly suggested we have dinner at her favorite Chinese restaurant.

Without giving it a second thought, we borrowed her roommate's car and drove several blocks downtown. After dinner, we emerged from the restaurant to find a group of people with sticks, brooms, pipes, and hammers, beating her roommate's car to a pulp. Stunned by the violence, we stood very still as it dawned on us that the car had Texas license plates. As her survival instincts kicked in, Mary Jane grabbed my hand and dragged me down the street.

Wearing a thin leather coat, I thought I might freeze to death before we made it back to her dorm. The frigid November wind howled between the buildings and I thought it was somehow appropriate as I swiped at the tears on my face. I told myself America would recover, but I'm not sure we ever did or ever will.

The musical revolution sweeping the country, led by Elvis Presley, Bob Dylan, The Beatles, and many others, seemed to express the anguish of a nation in turmoil. American youth, disillusioned and searching for meaning, found their voice in the wild gyrations of rock n' roll. As our parents looked on in horror, we abandoned ourselves to the primitive beat that spoke to us and for us. It was a true musical renaissance that underscored the history-making events of those days and echoed the birth pangs of change. Our school even allowed us to stay up late and order pizza when The Beatles appeared on *The Ed Sullivan Show*. Change was definitely coming, and even though I had suffered enough change to last a lifetime, I knew I had to step up to help those who needed change or be dragged, kicking and screaming into a very tumultuous future.

As I watched subsequent, deadly events unfold in churches and on college campuses, I wondered how much pain a person or a nation can withstand before dying of a broken heart.

CHAPTER 60

Meeting Juero

Age Eighteen

Thankfully, Christmas arrived quickly because I was looking forward to going to Mexico. Mother and I had decided we couldn't bear our first Christmas without Daddy at home, so when our friends in Mexico invited us down south, we gladly accepted. There just happened to be a pigeon shoot going on as well, but I was undecided about shooting without Daddy for the first time until I met Estella, the wife of a man I had often competed with, extending her small hand and saying, "I have long wanted to meet the girl who my husband admits is a better shot than he is." Her voice was deep and husky for such a tiny woman and I would later learn it was the result of many throat surgeries. They had removed one whole side of her neck in order to get all of the cancer, but you hardly noticed the scar because of her delightful manner and ethereal beauty. Her husband, Sergio, approached to ask if I planned to shoot, and offered me one of his guns.

Placing her small hand over mine, she said to her husband, "You men can redeem yourselves another time. I am enjoying her far too much to let her go." Turning back to me, she said, "Querida, I would like to introduce you to my cousin, Victor Hugo O'Farril Avila . . . Juero, to his friends and family. He is a great hunter like you and is most anxious to meet you. He is a very fiery, romantic boy, sort of dangerous, but in a good way. Do you know what I mean?"

I knew exactly what she meant—the kind of boy I was a sucker for—but I rationalized that I was saving myself for Darryl and immune to other boys. I was not prepared for the full-blown onslaught of a true Latino courtship, however, and I suddenly knew how women must have felt when faced with my father, Charles.

Juero was like a prince, straight out of a fairy tale, wielding his charms and wooing me in a million subtle ways. From the minute we met at the La Perla Club in Acapulco, he spun a protective web around us and treated me like a Dresden doll. No boy had ever behaved that way with me, and some weirdly feminine, Cinderella personality emerged from within me that I found both embarrassing and exhilarating. For a girl who had always been one of the guys, I found I liked being doted on and protected. When his older brother, Romulo, attempted a little harmless flirtation, Juero went for his brother's throat. Smiling good-naturedly, easygoing Romulo gently removed his brother's hand and said, "Easy, little brother. I was just playing." Turning to me, he said, "Con mucho gusto, señorita," and left his temperamental brother in peace.

Two brothers could hardly have been more different; Romulo was tall with very curly, almost red hair, a gift from his Irish father, whereas Juero was short with jet-black, straight hair like his Mexican mother. They both had beautiful green eyes, though Romulo's were twinkling and merry, while Juero's were intense and sometimes dangerous. From the very first night, Juero treated me in a proprietary manner and began to plan the holiday season for us. In his beautiful, lilting English, he enumerated all of the events that would need to take place. "First, you must meet my parents, of course. Then, my grandparents will have a big party to introduce you to Mexican society. Oh, my grandmother does not speak perfect English, so you should get in the habit of only speaking Spanish around her. My sister and Estella will take you shopping and to get your hair done."

As he took a breath, I exhaled and said, "I'll have to check with my mother." My head was spinning from the lengthy itinerary, and my meddling independent streak reared its ugly head and threatened to ruin my romantic interlude. I beat it back down and smiled sweetly as he said, "Leave your mother to me."

The rest was a blur of shops, hairdressers, parties, and introductions. His parents, warm and gracious, welcomed me with a party at their home in Acapulco. Next, his grandparents threw a lavish party to introduce me to their friends and I was amazed to find his grandfather, once the president of Mexico, a very down-to-earth gentleman. He had served as a general in the Mexican Revolution and had not forgotten his roots. I found them both charming and enjoyed practicing my Spanish with his grandmother, who was very tolerant of my frequent mistakes, saying, "At least, you try."

Delightful as it all was, especially the mariachi serenades, I had no idea how much trouble I was in until I talked to Estella near the end of our trip. Bursting with excitement, she exclaimed, "We are all so thrilled about your engagement. We will be family."

Feeling as if I might faint, something I had never done in my life, I gasped, "My what?" Estella repeated it first in Spanish and then in English. As I slumped to the couch, my mind racing, all I could think about was how ignorant an American could feel down here. I barely spoke two languages while most of my friends in Mexico spoke at least four or five. They were very European and sophisticated so I could only imagine that I had missed some pertinent sign or something had been terribly lost in translation. Wide-eyed, I stared at her as I said, "But he hasn't asked me to marry him."

Estella laughed in her husky way and said, "But what did you think it meant when he took you to meet his parents?"

Racking my brain, I said, "I don't know. I guess I thought everyone was just being really friendly."

Serious now, Estella said, "Querida, a Mexican boy never introduces a girl to his parents, and especially his grandparents, unless he intends to marry her."

Looking at her with pleading eyes, I said, "I didn't understand. What should I do?"

Shocked, she asked, "Don't you love Juero? Half the girls in Mexico City would kill to be with him."

Trying to be honest, I replied, "Estella, I don't know him. This has all been so sudden and I'm not even out of high school."

Reassured, Estella said, "Oh, don't worry. You can finish school and take your classes in Catholicism before the wedding." Suddenly, I felt like a calf being shoved down a shoot for branding and it took everything I had not to bolt.

When I returned to school, Juero faithfully called me almost every night and whenever I tried to tell him I wanted to go to college, he would brush it aside, saying, "You don't need college. You will be my wife." When I heard those words, even my Cinderella alter ego was ready to run for the hills. A Texas man might want to keep you barefoot and pregnant, but he usually had the good sense to keep it to himself if he valued his life.

All of my girlfriends were green with envy, saying how lucky I was to have found a rich prince. But somehow, it just didn't feel right, so I asked Mother what I should do. Thinking for a moment, she finally said, "Rita, most American boys can't deal with you and I'm not sure a Latin boy could tolerate your independence. Plus, you would be expected to raise your children in the Catholic Church and if there were problems, you might find it difficult to get out of the country. He's a charming but very volatile young man and his family is politically powerful. On a bright note, it will be several months before you graduate, and perhaps his ardor will cool by then."

That sounded right to me, and like Mama always said, "There's many a slip between the cup and the lip."

CHAPTER 61

Crossroads

Age Eighteen

My three best friends at school, Barbara, Robin, and Helen, were bright and level-headed for the most part, so I valued their opinions. They understood my need to go to college and graciously downplayed the good-looking, rich prince scenario. They stressed the benefits of college, pointing out that it would be good to have an education that I could fall back on if things didn't work out. And there could even be another revolution, and he could lose all of his money. After all, everyone knew communism was very popular with the Mexican youth and middle-class. I relayed all of these reasons to Juero, who was not impressed and always ended up saying, "We'll talk about it after you graduate."

I even resorted to telling him about Darryl, to which he answered, "He is in the past. I am your future." This was a boy not accustomed to hearing the word, "No," and I was a girl who ran from anything that would fence me in. As we continued our polite, suppressed battle of wills, only distance kept us from reaching the boiling point.

And then, there was the matter of Darryl. We seemed to have drifted apart now that he was on the rodeo circuit full-time. He called once or twice a month, whenever he could find a phone in the Podunk towns he rode in. Also, he knew I didn't like him to call when he was drinking, so that curtailed a lot of potential calls.

One night when he called, a name mix-up occurred that could not have happened at a worse time. The girl who answered the phone, thinking it was Juero, called him by that name. When I answered the phone, the first words out of his mouth were, "Who's Juero?"

Attempting to sound casual, I said, "A boy I met in Mexico." After a brief silence, Darryl asked, "Should I be worried?"

"No," I replied and asked, "What's wrong? I can hear something in your voice."

At first, I thought he was drunk, but now, I knew for sure, he was crying. "What's happened?" I asked again.

Finally, in a broken voice, he said, "My buddy was killed tonight in the bull riding event."

Stunned, I gasped, "What do you mean? How?"

He said, "It was goddamn awful. I'll never ride a bull again." And then, he wept like a small boy for the friend he couldn't save, while I listened and tried to offer what comfort I could.

Darryl was true to his word and never rode another bull. From that point on, he only rode saddle broncs, earning him the nickname Bronc. I was relieved because bulls were widow-makers. Darryl had a natural affinity with horses, so I didn't think they would hurt him too bad. That was one less thing to worry about.

But now, I had a new worry. Mother called infrequently and when she did, she sounded distracted. I knew the lawsuit was taking its toll on her, but this was something different. So I did what I had always done when I wanted to know what was going on; I called to talk to Rosie or Dorothy, who I knew would give me all of the juicy gossip whether it involved Zacaweista, Santa Rosa—the two portions of the ranch—or Vernon. Information went through those two women like a wildfire in dry pasture.

I was surprised when Rosie answered the phone. I asked, "Where are Mother and Joyce?"

"Your mother gave Joyce the week off," she huffed in an accusatory tone.

Baffled, I asked, "So, where is Mother? Is she drinking again?" Snorting, Rosie said, "They be drinking."

Even more confused, I asked, "Who are *they*?"

Revving up to her choir voice, Rosie said, "That would be the new accountant, who calls himself a 'Bible-thumping Baptist.' But girl, he got some bad juju. There's something not right about that man, taking advantage of a widow-woman like that."

That was my first introduction to Paul, the man who would soon become my new stepfather. I was not ready for this turn of events. Daddy and I had always planned to go on a photographic safari for my graduation present and I was still having a hard time picturing my graduation without him.

I tried to keep my voice level when Mother got on the phone and I asked, "Who's Paul?"

Sounding a little too chirpy, she answered, "Oh, he's the accountant our attorneys hired to examine the books. He's been a real godsend."

Trying not to sound judgmental, I replied, "It sounds like it."

Her tone going up a notch, she snapped, "What's that supposed to mean?"

I paused to gather my thoughts so we wouldn't end up in a fight as usual. I knew Mother deserved a break from the nightmare of our reality, but I couldn't bear the thought of someone replacing Daddy so soon. In the most conciliatory voice I could muster, I answered, "It means I'm glad you have some help. How long will he be there?"

Sounding chirpy again, she said, "Oh, he'll have to be here quite often over the next few months. There's a lot of work to be done."

I swallowed the criticism on my tongue and said, "Well, I hope he'll be able to take some of the burden off of you. I know how hard it must be."

Naturally assuming I meant the pressure of the lawsuit and preparing for our move, she was appeased by my understanding and said, "It's hard, but I've got help now. I'll be fine. Don't you worry."

I assured her I wouldn't, but I was very worried because I knew one important truth about my mother. She couldn't be without a man, and under these bitter conditions, I feared what kind of man she might reach out to in desperation. If she had not had to bury herself in the insurmountable problems we faced, perhaps she would have met a nice man through her friends. Such was not the case, and a new stone was thrown, creating an ever-widening ripple effect that would shatter many lives in the near future.

CHAPTER 62

Leaving the Ranch

Age Eighteen

The dreaded day finally arrived and now I sat by the pond on the hill, my secret place, saying my goodbyes. I wasn't sure if you could die of a broken heart, but I felt like you could. We had just buried Pa, Daddy's father, so the last of my beloved men had left me to journey on alone. I consoled myself with the thought that they were in a better place and I certainly wouldn't have wanted Daddy to witness this sad exodus. He had suffered enough heartbreak, and I was glad he had been spared this last humiliation.

I had decided that lawsuits were the most cold-blooded weapons people could use against one another and vowed to never shake hands with that devil again. And it wasn't just Mother and me losing our home; Johnny had fired most of Daddy's loyal employees, so they, too, were being forced to leave their homes and uproot their families. I had grown up with these people and we shared a multitude of memories. Like so many others on the ranch, they had kept me safe and helped shape the person I would become. Now, I would probably never see them again and I felt ashamed because we had let them down. Without Daddy, it all seemed so futile and empty; I had lost heart for the battle. I just wanted to find a peaceful, safe place where I could escape the constant conflict and pain.

My attorneys, shooting straight for the heart, threw down the gauntlet they knew would force me to accept the challenge. Elton, playing bad cop, asked, "Did Buster raise a quitter? Would he want you to lay down and let them take this ranch?"

George, playing the good cop, wrapped his arm around my shoulders as I hung my head and wept softly. I was bone-tired, but sometimes you've got to bite the bullet and reach for your last ounce of strength in order to get across the finish line. Daddy had always said, "Give me a horse with heart over talent, any day." I wasn't a quitter so I promised Elton I would fight the good fight until the bitter end.

Now, as I sat on my bench for the last time, I thought of all the animals that would be affected by our departure. I had no idea what would happen to most of them because we could only take the poodles and my two horses. Mother had given her horses to Aunt Avis, who would also keep mine until we got settled somewhere. I wondered what would happen to all of the other horses, the hunting dogs, the peacocks, the squirrels, the birds, the monkeys, my little burro Pepe, my deer, Bambi, and Bandit, my raccoon, not to mention the ducks, geese, rabbits, and chickens. I was thinking it was a good thing Daddy had made me return the baby elephant Kirk Johnson had given me. The poor little thing would have probably ended up in a zoo, rather than safe and happy on the Johnson's elephant reserve. I knew we had let them down too, all of our creature friends who had been my faithful companions, especially in the really bad times. I couldn't bear to contemplate what their fate might be, so I turned my thoughts to Darryl and Juero.

Darryl wasn't ready to settle down any more than I was, so he would continue to rodeo while I went to college. I just hoped he would find himself out there, rather than lose himself like so many did. Juero had forgiven me for rebuffing his proposal and had made it clear he did not want to burn any bridges. I was brutally honest and told him I had four years of college ahead and no idea what I would feel or who I would be at the end of that time. I knew what a valiant effort it took to acquiesce to such an undefined arrangement, and I appreciated his valor greatly.

A humorous twist of fate had recently made me the recipient of several proposals of marriage from various counts and dukes throughout Europe. When my attorneys presented the offers to me, I laughed for the first time in an age, saying, "Why would I want to marry some count or duke I don't even know?"

Looking deadly serious, Elton replied, "The title."

Guffawing, I said, "The title? A title means nothing to me. What would they get out of it?"

With a wry smile, Elton said, "Money."

Laughing again, I said, "I don't have any money."

He cocked an eyebrow and wagged his finger, saying, "Ah, but you will. You will be a very rich young lady and a real catch."

I frowned as I thought about the implications in his statement and finally said, "I don't know if that would be such a good thing. I want someone to love me for me."

Looking at me sadly, Elton said, "Spoken like a true granddaughter. Those are almost the exact words Electra Waggoner wrote in her will. I sincerely hope you have better luck than she did."

The move from the ranch had just about sent Mother over the edge and she seemed almost manic now. Johnny Biggs had been heard to say he would bulldoze Zacaweista if he had his way, which lit a fire in Mother that raged out of control until the day she died. Determined to never let him destroy or get his hands on anything of Daddy's, she ripped up the carpet and anything else she could until the house was nothing but a shell. As she stared at the poor carcass, she breathed a sigh of satisfaction, knowing she had salvaged all she could. She had no control over what Johnny did to the rest of Zacaweista, but she had at least saved the essence of our home. As she realized it was really finished and that she might never set foot on the ranch again, her face crumpled as she turned away to hide her tears. The attorneys had informed us that we could be looking at years of litigation because there were between thirty-five and forty-five serious contestants in the lawsuit now, including the State of Texas.

I intended to keep a very low profile in order to avoid the notoriety our little family problem had attracted. My last year at Newport, the school had to hire special security guards to prevent reporters and fortune hunters from sneaking onto the grounds. I was a loner at heart anyway, but now I was even more leery of publicity and hoped I could somehow melt into the throngs of people in the city. Mother had decided to move us back to Dallas, where I would attend college at Southern Methodist University. My dear friend, Layton, was already taking charge in his usual manner and was determined to do whatever it took to lift my spirits. Ever the big brother, he offered me a safe haven and I was glad to accept it.

I tried not to obsess on the final outcome, consoling myself with the knowledge that there was a greater Inheritance than the one I was fighting for. The two things they could never take away were my identity and my faith. Even though I had been told I was no longer a part of this family, I knew who I was and didn't need their acceptance to have a sense of myself.

My fathers had given me that gift and no one could take it away or tarnish it with lies or half-truths. Like the title of a favorite book of poetry, my fathers were too gentle to be wolves. They had their weaknesses, to be sure, but they were not consumed by greed or lust for power. They were successful men, in the truest sense of the word, because they loved well and were well loved. Would that we could all make such a claim, for there is no greater epitaph than Love.

And so, as I gently pulled up my roots and said my tearful farewells, I thought to myself, "I don't know where the road will lead me, but I know who I follow so I am not afraid."

EPILOGUE

Eight years later, after going all the way to the Texas Supreme Court, the lawsuit was settled in Bucky's favor. For many years afterward, he ran the ranch in a way that would have made his father proud. In 2016, the ranch was sold and now only the legend remains. My brother may have gotten the ranch and the money, but I am the keeper of the memories; they are safely tucked away in my heart, where neither people nor time can steal them away.

I did go to college like Daddy wanted and graduated with a double major in psychology and social work and a minor in sociology. I worked for the Fort Worth Welfare Department as a child abuse counselor and as a supervisor at the first autism clinic in Texas. I later worked as a behavioral therapist at the Denton State School for the Mentally Retarded and as an employment counselor at the Texas Employment Commission.

My life took a sudden turn when I went to seminary at the Unity School of Christianity in Kansas City, Missouri, and graduated in 1983, as a licensed, ordained Unity Minister. I served as the senior minister of the Unity Church of Denton, and then as an associate minister at the Unity Church of Dallas.

When my mother made her transition in 1986, I took over the family farm and grew wheat and cotton until I decided to sell the land over conservation concerns.

Today, I am retired and living a free and peaceful life in New Mexico, the Land of Enchantment. My beautiful daughter and I enjoy a life of simple grace far from the flamboyant ranch where I spent my childhood, and yet, every time I see a bird flying close to the ground, I say a silent prayer for its soft landing, and give thanks, again, for my own.

Genesis 4:5 ~ *"Ye meant it for evil, but God meant it for good."*

John 19:11 ~ *"You would have no power over me unless it had been given to you from above."*

Matthew 25:34 ~ *"Come, O blessed of my father, inherit the Kingdom prepared for you from the foundation of the world."*

DEDICATIONS

To my beloved daughter, Rena Mielle, so that she will know the truth about her family.

To my parents, Lu and Bus, who, in spite of their illnesses, taught me to love life, have faith, and believe in magic.

To my father, Charles, for always putting my best interests before his own. To Mama and Avis, for always being my light in the darkness.

To my surrogate mothers, Miss Mandy, Grace, and Joyce, for giving me the best of themselves. And most of all, to those who gave life to the ranch with their blood, sweat, and tears.

ACKNOWLEDGEMENTS

I would like to thank Anne G. Devlin at the Max Gartenburg Literary Agency for her belief in my book and her persistence in helping me to get it published.

Thanks to Jeannine Seymour for her superb editing and encouragement.

I would also like to thank my daughter, Rena Mielle, for her help throughout the editing and publishing process.

www.ingramcontent.com/pod-product-compliance
Lightning Source LLC
LaVergne TN
LVHW091134080826
845145LV00008B/2142

* 9 7 8 0 8 7 5 6 5 9 6 1 9 *